The Lessons of Failure

ANDREW ROBERTSON

The Lessons of failure

Cases and comments on consumer product innovation

MACDONALD *London and New York*

MACDONALD TECHNICAL
AND SCIENTIFIC

PO Box No. 2LG, St Giles House,
49/50 Poland Street, London W1A 2LG

ISBN 0 356 04386 x

First published 1974

Printed and bound in Great Britain by
W. & G. Baird Limited, Antrim, N. Ireland

Contents

Acknowledgments

The author would like to thank all those organisations and individuals who helped with the compilation of this collection of case histories, but who are in no way responsible for any errors or omissions.

In particular he is grateful for the personal help of Mr Michael Colston, Dr Jacob Bronowski, Mr Mark Boxer, Professor Harry Henry, Mr Vernon Thomas and Miss Eirlys Roberts.

He would also like to thank the Consumers' Association, the *Economist* and Messrs W. H. Allen for permission to reproduce material.

There were many other individuals who gave a lot of time in interviews and correspondence but who prefer to remain anonymous. They are already aware of the value of their help and the gratitude with which it was received.

Select bibliography

Belbin, R. M., *Quality Calamities and their Management Implications* (BIM, 1970).

Borrie, G., and Diamond, A. L., *The Consumer, Society and the Law* (Penguin Books, 1964; MacGibbon & Kee, 1966).

Cole, H. R., and Diamond, A. L., *The Consumer and the Law* (Co-operative Union, 1960).

Egan, Bowes, *The Customer and the Law* (Constable, 1969).

Fulop, C., *Consumers in the Market* (Institute of Economic Affairs, 1967).

—— *Competition for Consumers* (André Deutsch for IEA, 1964).

Gundrey, E., *Your Money's Worth* (Penguin Books, 1962).

—— *At Your Service* (Penguin Books, 1964).

—— *Value for Money* (Zenith Books, 1967).

—— *A Foot in the Door* (Muller, 1965).

Knox, F., *Consumers and the Economy* (Harrap, 1969).

Leaper, W. J., *New Trade Descriptions Law* (Business Books, 1968).

Major, W. T., *Sale of Goods* (Macdonald & Evans, 1965).

Martin, J., and Smith, G. W., *The Consumer Interest* (Pall Mall Press, 1968).

Masters, D., *The Intelligent Buyer's Guide to Sellers* (Consumers' Union of the US, 1965).

Millar, R., *The Affluent Sheep* (Longmans, 1963).

Molony, J. T. (Chairman), *Final Report of the Committee on Consumer Protection*, Cmnd 1781 (HMSO, 1962).

Newman, J. W. (ed.), *On Knowing the Consumer* (John Wiley, 1966).

Roberts, E., *Consumers* (Watts, 1966).

Tench, D., *The Law for Consumers* (Consumers' Association, 1962).

INTRODUCTION

The blind spot

The idea for this book is derived from Ernest Dichter's justly celebrated *Strategy of Desire*, in which are to be found most, if not all, of the logic and philosophy of the 'father' of motivation research. Published in 1960 *Strategy of Desire* contains his comments on human responses to objects, to products. For those who have not read the book Dr Dichter's descriptions of 'the soul of things', which is the title of one of his chapters, will have reached them both secondhand and garbled, in all probability. Any intelligent reader of the original will have recognized the sensitivity and correctness of his extraordinary and unprecedented approach to inanimate objects and their significance for human beings.

It is Dr Dichter's belief that the underlying feelings which people have about objects (for instance, that coffee poured from an old and battered pot tasted better than the same pre-brewed liquid from a shining new container) can be understood and exploited in marketing, in politics, and in other situations where one set of people wants to influence another.

The record shows that motivation research has had its successes. Nothing has been reported about its failures, if any, but the fact remains that, with or without motivation research or any other marketing technique or battery of techniques, there have been some serious marketing failures. No one likes to admit failure, so it should not surprise us that we know so little of its circumstances, not to mention the reasons for it. We can hazard a guess that product innovation failure occurs because, for some reason, the consuming public refuses to buy it in quantities sufficient for the manufacturer to stay in business.

Obvious enough, but it is possible, as we have seen recently, for a large and sophisticated company such as E. I. Du Pont de Nemours to lose as much as $250 million before discovering that this was happening. The Corfam story, which is a consumer product innovation failure as shattering in its own way as the Rolls-Royce RB-211, is retold here with as much detail as the company allowed. It is one of eight case-histories of failure or lack of success, compiled with the object of deriving some ideas that may lead to a better understanding of the consumer goods market as far as innovation is concerned.

The justification for this approach is simply that failure cases may conceivably confer more wisdom than those of success, and there are more than enough of those about, including the sixty or seventy (depending on how you count them) in the celebrated text, *The Sources of Invention*, by Professor John Jewkes and his collaborators Sawers and Stillerman (Macmillan, 2nd edition, 1969). Failure studies can be numbered on the fingers of one hand. They would include, of course, John Brooks's *The Fate of the Edsel.* According to Martin Mayer's *Madison Avenue USA*, two theses and a dissertation were written on the subject of Columbia University's Bureau of Applied Social Research and its work for the Ford Motor Company on the marketing of the Edsel, but before it was realised what an awful flop the car was going to be.

Ernest Dichter himself, who advised Chrysler on the Plymouth, typically attributed the Edsel's failure to win the affections of the American public to the fact that its shape did not have the essential 'symbolic significance' of the car. The car is 'a penetrating instrument' and therefore has 'considerable significance as a phallic symbol'. The Edsel's nose, unlike Cleopatra's, was too short, in other words.

Was this the whole explanation in reality? John Brooks gives many more in his study, some of which we refer to later on, but one has only to think of all the successful models of car which have been decidedly unphallic in shape (the Rolls-Royce, the Volkswagen, the Mini-Minor, to name a trio) to see that the good doctor may not have the full explanation for the failure of that car at that time, let alone all the others.

Elsewhere in his book, also with reference to cars, he mentions what he calls 'the final motivation' which is that 'we want to be successful as buyers. We don't want to have the feeling that we have been made fools of, that we did not shop or buy wisely.' This comment is much more to the point as far as this book is concerned, for in it we are dealing with material satisfaction, the feeling of the customer that he has been fairly dealt with, been given good value for money. For this reason the first case-study is not one of out and out failure, but of partial failure, poor customer relations, and their interconnection.

There is an inescapable feeling that some businessmen, and that includes executives engaged in selling, cannot completely resist the P. T. Barnum attitude, that 'there is one (sucker) born every minute'. That there is plenty of evidence to support this attitude is clear from the success of doorstep pedlars, crooked insurance brokers, and others who specialize in parting the public from its money without giving anything substantial in return. But it can be a fatal position to adopt in any business based on long-term profitability and growth. Here there is much less available evidence to go on, but one or two cases in this small collection suggest that in the long run customer dissatisfaction will cancel out any amount of hard selling and glossy publicity.

That is why the title of this introduction is 'The Blind Spot'. The author was for more than a dozen years a contributor to two weekly columns specializing in consumer advice and has recently spent five years studying innovation. From all this it has emerged that, for all the sophistication of their methods, marketing men have still not filled in a blind spot about the consumer, and that is his or her response not just to the apparatus of marketing, as detected by research and analysis, but to the product over time.

One reason for this absence of long-term response references may be that marketing in a large number of consumer goods areas has chosen to follow the policy of annual 'facelifts' particularly in cars and other consumer durables. With so many product changes it becomes impossible to trace any long-term feelings about the original product, even when the item has been remodelled for the fifth time leaving the basic product substantially the same.

However that may be, and it is arguable that the public is now becoming too mature for such gimmickry to pay off much longer, we also have to accept the fact that a measure of rationality has crept back into consumer choice, thanks to the activities of such organizations as the Consumers' Association and the late Consumer Council. It is not too far-fetched to surmise that a lot of the hostility displayed for the 'consumer movement' arose from the resentment of business people ill-advised enough to feel that their beloved suckers were about to become too clever for comfort.

This hostility was most apparent when *Which?* first began to publish comparative test results in 1957. Manufacturers were not unnaturally apprehensive lest their products should be unlucky in the draw and the Consumers' Association should purchase through proxies some unfortunately poor examples of their output. There must also have been some who knew well enough that their products were inadequate, and joined the chorus of opposition as a form of offensive defence.

Now the hostility has appeared in the open. The Government has closed the Consumer Council, established in 1963 by a Conservative administration in response to the findings of the Molony Committee on Consumer Protection. The public relations and advertising journal *Campaign* (15 December 1970) quoted a Canadian advertising agent Ernie Baltz (or Balts, they spelled it both ways) as saying that 'consumerism' may turn out to be as evil as McCarthyism. That exaggeration is a reminder of the phrase *Which ?*-hunt coined by the opponents of open and honest marketing.

It is this writer's belief that, in the long run, the firms which survive and prosper are the straight dealing, value for money firms. Marks and Spencer do not seem to have suffered from their policy of quality control on behalf of their customers. Nor have they suffered more than a little from the stupid and selfish abuse by a minority of customers of their generous policy of no-questions-asked exchange of unsatisfactory goods. In general the consumer-oriented policies of Marks and Spencer have paid off handsomely.

The point of this short book then is to hammer home, mainly by the use of case-histories, mostly new in the sense of not having been published before at any length or even at all, the crucial importance of gaining an understanding of the consumer and his needs

Understanding the consumer

Lord Cole, a former chairman of Unilever, once said in a speech that he and his company understood the British housewife. This was at a time when the Glasgow Consumer Group had issued a bulletin showing the confusion of prices and packet sizes of washing powders in the supermarkets in and around their city. The members of this group were angry at the deliberate confusion, as they saw it, created by the detergent manufacturers (Unilever and Proctor & Gamble were the two companies most involved) as a means of selling more powder for more money. Now while it is true that a monopolist (or as in this case duopolist) hardly needs to worry about his 'image', as the consumer's only weapon, abstention, is not available, it is undesirable for a well-known businessman not to match words with deeds. Hence the eventual regulation of pack size, weight, and pricing by the detergent makers under the encouraging eye of the then Board of Trade.[1] Even Unilever, with its sharp marketing edge, had revealed a blind spot.

Such gaps in the understanding of the consumer are far from rare. Sometimes, of course, they arise from crude commercial motives that dictate the unscrupulous treatment of consumers by entrepreneurs, usually a short-run situation, such as a phoney carpet sale, or a short, sharp direct-selling campaign to unload substandard goods, or a so-called sale of so-called bankrupt stock. As long as the unscrupulous seller sticks to short-run operations and does not break the law too flagrantly he knows that the ill-will accumulated by his operation can do him no lasting harm. This book is not addressed to such people, who probably do not read books anyway, but to businessmen with long-run intentions who do not want unwittingly to dissipate public goodwill. That they do is abundantly clear from numerous examples, but perhaps at this stage of the argument a few figures, albeit derivative and not original, are required.

According to James Albrecht, writing in the American journal *Research Management* (Spring, 1970), 'for every 100 *new* products offered to the trade, only 23 reach eventual acceptance'. In 1968 9,450 new or *new* items appeared on supermarket shelves in the United States. One-fifth of them achieved their planned sales targets. The rest were withdrawn. It has been said elsewhere (by the National Industrial Conference Board in the United States) that of every 100 *new* products put on sale 90 per cent are withdrawn from sale within three years of launch. A high proportion of them are withdrawn even earlier. An advertising man, Robin Wight, in a racy new book called *The Day the Pigs Refused to be Driven to Market* (Hart-Davis-MacGibbon 1972), comments on the 80 per cent new product rejection rate that it is a symptom of social dissatisfaction with 'mass conumption', that people are tiring of possessions, feeling surrounded by muddle, not richness of choice. His percentage figure and his conclusions are drawn from the American scene.

No comparable figures appear to exist for the British market, but the supposition is that, while the percentage of failure may not be as

1. This was also, of course, the origin of 'Square deal' Surf, the surviving 'cheap' washing powder.

high as in the United States, it is high enough to make some form of inquiry aimed at reducing it worth while. An additional fact of relevance here is that, generally speaking, a 'failed' product is costlier than a success because firms are inclined to go on spending on it in the hope of eventual success and a pay-off.

Anyone in business sceptical of the value of either the figures or the argument has a fingertip test he can make. He should have a look at his own firm's new product record over the past three years. Check off the successes and failures and their relative profits and losses. If the former outweigh the latter in financial terms you have done well. If the former outweigh the latter in actual numbers you do not need to read on.

Product innovation can be an ambiguous phrase, hence the use of *new* and new. The ballpoint pen, when it was first introduced to the public, was genuinely new. Most other so-called innovations are *new* in the sense that the marketing men use the word in copy and on packages. Some familiar product reaching the end of its upswing in the product cycle has been given a short-term boost with a superficial 'improvement', a 'facelift', a 'new image'. Strictly speaking this is not innovation, at least not of a serious and lasting kind. Some people might refer to it as gimmickry. Apparently there are sections of the public which do not like it, just as there are also sections which appear to accept it. Nevertheless, if we believe the Albrecht and NICB figures (and there are others), even this does not pay off as frequently as its instigators seem to expect. Although it is far less costly, in cash terms, than what we may term 'real innovation', what the cost of failed gimmickry might be in other terms, of goodwill or good public relations, is too conjectural to deserve more than a passing mention.

As Jacob Schmookler has pointed out in *Invention and Economic Growth* (Chapter IX of the 1966 Harvard edition) innovation for consumers, where there is not a completely new product, takes the form of changes in cost and quality of existing products. Four combinations are possible within these limits: improved quality at the same cost, improved quality at higher cost, lower cost with the same quality, or lower cost with lower quality. Consumers, as far as they are aware of marketing tactics, also experience what may be termed *apparent* improvements in quality at the same or higher cost. The term apparent must be used because there are certain products which, without chemical analysis or other expert investigation not normally available to consumers, can claim to be 'new' and 'improved' or both when they are neither, except in the restricted sense that they have been subjected to what marketing people sometimes call a 'relaunch'.

In this not uncommon situation a company's marketing methods may be called in question by organized consumer opinion, such as exists now in a number of industrialized countries or by official bodies such as the US Food and Drugs Administration. Generally speaking the purpose of consumers' associations is advisory, a service to subscribing members aimed at clarifying for them the problems of choosing among a multitude of goods for sale where the claims made in sales literature, advertisements, over the counter, or by other means are of a technical nature beyond the informed criticism of individuals, for example, 'kills all known germs', 'has more cleansing power', 'the sort doctors prefer', and so forth.

The hostility felt by some marketing executives and businessmen for consumer organizations and for official intervention seems to arise to a large extent from a feeling that their activities are in some way an interference with the traditional business of selling by all means not hitherto forbidden by law. It is an instructive reflection that this century has seen, especially in the past ten years, a significant growth in protective consumer legislation. Public opinion has compelled the lawmakers to act in defence of the individual consumer on a number of grounds, beginning with health and proceeding slowly via various forms of deception to safety and now, in Britain at least, to misdescription and false pricing. The one-sided battle under the flag of *caveat emptor*[1] is no longer the seller's prerogative, the buyer also has some weapons even and some allies now.

Costs and benefits

The lessons for the commercial firm over this period might be summed up as honesty is the best long-term policy. It always was when there were far fewer opportunities for deception (the main areas were food and drink and textile products), but it is even more important now. In certain consumer goods industries it has become simplicity itself to hoodwink the public about quality. Even now companies are still issuing guarantees which are worded in such a

1. It has been contended that the appropriate Latin tag would now be *caveat venditor* (cf. Wills, G. C., 'Consumption and Welfare: *Caveat Emptor* to *Caveat Vendor* (*sic*)', in Tillett, A., *et al.*, *Management Thinkers*, Penguin, 1970) but there is a long way to go yet before this can be wholly true.

way as to deprive buyers of their common law and statutory rights if they sign and return them. In spite of the exposure of this practice well over a decade ago by the Consumer Advisory Council of the British Standards Institution (forerunner of the short-lived Consumer Council), after which some well-known British firms agreed to reword their warranties, the practice persists. Have the executives responsible for such a policy in their company studied the costs and benefits of it? It probably never occurred to them that there were any costs.

The company with a reputation for straight and open dealing with the public hardly needs the kind of public relations which amounts to systematic whitewashing. The company's behaviour speaks for itself, as the Marks and Spencer case confirms. Hackneyed the example may be, but it is all the more impressive because a generation ago that company had a reputation for hard and ruthless buying in order to be able to command mass markets. Now the company is looked upon as exemplary in its attention to quality control and for its generous attitude to dissatisfied customers. Evidently here is one business that prospered without recourse to confusing or misleading claims, trimming of quality, or other questionable tactics of the kind condemned in the Consumer Council's *The First Seven Years: 1963–1970*, a summary of the continuing struggle to obtain a fairer deal for shoppers. It now reads like an obituary.

The question to be raised here, among others, is whether such tactics are really essential to the profitable operation of a business or indeed whether they do not in the long run do more harm than good. But the other side of the coin is the genuine misunderstanding of consumer needs, which is almost as common as exaggerated claims and over-optimistic advertising, to put it nicely. In short, not only must the marketing executive ask 'is my hyperbole really necessary' (to which the full answer is not the obvious one: 'others do it, so we must'), but he must also take care to see that product innovation is both genuine and needed, and therefore an addition to real consumer satisfaction.

That word 'needed' raises some difficulties which are perhaps best resolved by resorting to examples. An obvious one in Britain is the refrigerator. Twenty years ago it was a rarity in British homes. The ownership percentage in 1956 was a mere seven. One reason was that British men (who have to be persuaded, not their wives) appeared to believe that a refrigerator was only of use in the summer (with the usual British suggestion that the country does not really have a summer, anyway). Manufacturers were irritably resigned to the seasonal nature of refrigerator sales. In winter sales were negligible, storage space was costly as the appliances could not be stored collapsed and took up a lot of room, and also the plant had to be kept running for the sake of economy. With an alternative product like a washing machine (also mainly a box with attachments), given that it had a reasonable level of winter sales, that problem was mitigated to some extent. But a cold, wet summer meant a poor offtake of stock and a sharp rise in warehouse charges and work-in-progress.

The answer lay in convincing the British family that it needed a refrigerator as a food store all the year round. The leading makers set up the Domestic Refrigerator Development Committee (Dordec) and began a publicity campaign aimed at putting across the idea of the refrigerator as something more than a source of ice and cold drinks. A piece of luck was that about this time the frozen food business was beginning in Britain, led by Bird's-Eye. The two growth curves of sales are interestingly related.[1] Suffice it to say that by 1970 ownership figures for refrigerators, with a growing population, had reached 66 per cent. There are many homes that would function far less efficiently today without a refrigerator. It has become a necessity for some, a useful rather than a prestige possession for others and, if it were cheaper and could be accommodated in the small dwellings that are so common in present crowded urban conditions, could become a universal article of furniture, as it is in the United States.

Hindsight

These commments are, of course, endowed with the wisdom of hindsight, as indeed are all the case-histories in this book. The point of them is that they offer lessons that may be applied as foresight, and it is extremely interesting to notice how much might have been learnt from the mistakes of the recent past but apparently has not been. One reason may be that it is not easy to study the sequence of product innovation without setting out the main facts and looking at them against the social and economic background of their time.

The refrigerator case (which is not studied in this collection in

1. The figures may be compared in Tables 3 and 27 (pp. 36 and 39 respectively) of *Bird's Eye Annual Review 1971*.

detail) serves to illustrate another example of mistiming in the processed food industry. Case 3 sets out the history of the Irish Sugar Company's attempt to innovate freeze-dried foods in the United Kingdom market, and attempts to explain what went wrong. A contributory factor in the eventual failure of this first attempt and the compromise arrived at with H. J. Heinz was surely the simultaneous growth of refrigerator ownership, giving people the opportunity to stock frozen foods which, in that period, seemed to be preferred to freeze-dried foods. Apparently no one in Erin Foods ever studied refrigerator ownership figures or they would have seen the danger implicit in that trend. This kind of 'blind spot' is not as uncommon as it should be, and arises from Levitt's 'myopia', the inability or refusal to recognize what business a company is really in. Erin Foods were inevitably competing in the whole of the food-processing industry. Every alternative process was competitive, but they apparently thought that they were in freeze-drying and had at least a temporary monopoly. Students of Professor Theodore Levitt's *Marketing Myopia* will recognize the symptoms (see *Harvard Business Review*, July–August, 1960).

In the domestic appliance business there are several instances of poor timing, one of which, dishwashers, is looked at in Case 2. The late Sir Charles Colston was a pioneer in the sense that he tried to innovate the first British-designed washing-up machine and found the going very hard indeed. At the time he seemed to believe that an important factor in his lack of success was a *Which?* report containing numerous adverse criticisms about performance. But at that time ownership had reached, after two years of selling (1958–60) no more than 0·5 per cent. True, the half-million readers of the Consumers' Association journal were not going to rush to buy any kind of dishwasher after seeing their July 1960 report. But what could explain the lack of dynamic growth before the report was published? Was *Which?* being made a scapegoat? Subsequent study of women's attitudes (and men's) suggests that there are acceptance problems that might have been exacerbated by that early report but were not created by it.

This introduction is not intended to be a summary of the book, but one or two further examples of misunderstanding of the consumer's needs will serve to complete the notion of the 'blind spot'. A notable and impressive instance occurs in the history of the Du Pont leather substitute Corfam. It is all the more striking and illustrative (and further details are given in Case 6) because of the immense care and trouble the company took over user tests, market analysis, and attitude surveys. If ever a new product was planned using all available techniques it was this one. But one plus turned out in the end to be a minus. Corfam was 'too good' for most of its market. It lasted too long and cost too much, and as a consequence lost a lot of its potential market to cheaper, less durable, and apparently less suitable materials.

Breakages Ltd

There is a sturdy legend about consumer goods, assisted in its perpetuation by Bernard Shaw in his preface to *The Apple Cart.* He invented a sinister firm called Breakages Ltd whose task it was to make sure that nothing was ever built to last, because there is too little turnover and therefore too little profit in goods that will not wear out or break down. We now call this 'quality' built-in or planned obsolescence. We have all heard the story of the everlasting match, allegedly suppressed by the Swedes, and of the long-life bulb that no lamp manufacturer will make,[1] not to mention the nylon stockings designed to ladder after two or three wearings.

But there is a true story about an almost everlasting sock that supports the Shavian belief in the unprofitability of durability. The Essinay sock (Case 8), manufactured by Simpson, Wright and Low of Sutton-in-Ashfield, Nottinghamshire (hence S-in-A), was made of spun nylon, that is nylon staple chopped to short lengths and spun after the fashion of wool. When new its appearance and handle were remarkably like those of wool, but this sock did not wear into holes. Without any kind of repair they were known to have lasted for four or five years and more, depending on the intensity of use and the habits of the wearer. They pilled (the surface fibres rolled into lumps), discoloured, and even shrunk a fraction from felting, but they did not wear out.

They were suppressed not by the makers or by the sock knitters, but by the retail trade. It is not enough, then, merely to aim at pleasing the ultimate consumer. In product innovation life is not that simple, a point that was by no means ignored by Du Pont. The retail end of product innovation is of crucial importance in the acceptance and survival of a new product, as even the most inexperienced marketing

1. Except for the Crompton-Parkinson 2,000-hour lamp, of course.

man knows. But it is still a trap for the manufacturer who fails to give it sufficient attention of the right kind. The retailer, from the head buyer through to the assistant confronting the customer, is a complex creature, coming between the innovator and the individuals for whom he supposes he is working. It is no wonder that some appliance manufacturers like John Bloom found an important sales advantage in doorstep demonstrations and direct sales (see Case 7). Direct selling could have saved the 'long-life' sock.

Unfortunately for the improvement of general knowledge of consumer reaction, most doorstep contact appears to have taken the form of the hard and crooked sell (see, for example, Elizabeth Gundrey's *A Foot in the Door*, Muller, 1965). In such circumstances the customer is more of a victim than a willing buyer, which deprives the maker of the goods of any 'feedback' of consumer reaction. In any case, the goods will rarely be of high quality and the maker will not expect repeat sales. Nor will he, on the whole, be in the least bit interested in the hostility evoked by his salesmen's tactics.

In general, therefore, the manufacturer tends to be remote from the ultimate consumer, which explains the immense proliferation of research agencies purporting to offer to businesses insights into the psychological behaviour of consumers. They range from old-style market research, largely based on interviewing, to the more high-flown technique of Dr Dichter's motivation research loosely anchored to the work of Freud and Adler. There are numerous success stories about the work of Dr Ernest Dichter, the motivation theory pioneer, and his followers. Little or nothing has been published about the long-term results of their apparent successes. There is a good case for insisting that such revelations, like case-studies of commercial failure with innovation, can do more good than harm, even to the consultants concerned (who will most probably know the facts, but prefer to keep them to themselves).

The marketing man in a manufacturing company making consumer goods, whatever his title (in the smaller firm it is frequently managing director), can do a great deal to teach himself about consumer acceptance and long-term goodwill leading to a rising market share, before spending anything on consultancy. It was easier to do in the past than it is now, because the manufacturer was once closer to his market than he can be nowadays when selling nationally has to be his ultimate aim, with the eventual expectation of exports. The method is to look upon the customer, to use the words of Professor Tom Burns,[1] as a 'source' and not as a 'sink'.

In other words, not as a means of getting rid of stock but as a fount of ideas for acceptance and improvement (which is what all that interviewing is ostensibly about). The sources lie to hand. They are the publications of the Consumers' Association, the late Consumer Council, the local consumer groups, the consumer columns of newspapers, the letters to the editor, the Weights and Measures inspectorate's many bulletins, Citizen's Advice Bureaux reports (where there are any), and, of course, the Retail Trading-Standards Association. In short all the existing apparatus of response by the consumers and their advisors and defenders. In this apparently enemy country lie valuable mines of information.

What will be difficult to find are case-studies of success and failure containing object lessons that may guide future decision-making. In this book a selection is offered as a pioneering attempt to fill that gap.

1. Burns and Stalker, *The Management of Innovation* (Tavistock Press, 1961).

CASE

1 *Is the customer always wrong?*

According to the conventional wisdom of British industry there is an inbred hostility between production and marketing. The production department makes something without sufficient attention to market requirements and then the marketing department is expected to go out and sell it. If and when the marketing men fail the blame rests with them.

In the past few years, according to general belief, British industry has become 'marketing oriented', and now puts the horse before the cart. Production takes its orders from marketing and as a result the 'marketing edge' of some British firms has been thoroughly sharpened.

Through the eyes of a customer whether this claim is true or not does not seem to matter. From the outside viewpoint the manufacturing company, in some instances anyway, bears the aspect of a conspiracy to sell something and see that it stays sold, no matter what. The motor manufacturing industry has provided some dramatic examples of this attitude and may now be finding that in the long run it does not pay.

To be specific, take the case of the Vauxhall Viva, a low-priced saloon launched on the British market in 1964. According to the *Financial Times* (16 September 1970) 'it filled a gap in the market' and at the peak of its popularity 'Vauxhall captured 13 per cent of UK domestic sales'. Thereafter sales reached a plateau and, after the launch of the rival Ford Escort in 1968 and the Hillman Avenger in 1970, the Vauxhall market share had slipped to around 9 per cent. In 1970 it was only 7 per cent (*The Times*, 23 January 1971).

One probable reason for this decline was competition, but another was almost certainly poor quality and reliability. What follows is an actual account of one customer's dealings with Vauxhall and its London dealer Henlys Ltd during approximately six months of ownership of a new Vauxhall Viva, from October 1968 to April 1969. At the end of this period the owner, weary of breakdowns and services, lengthy correspondence and even bills for repairs under warranty, simply left the car at another dealer's and traded it in. This was a slightly less dramatic gesture than setting fire to it as one dissatisfied owner did with his Ford Anglia (*The Guardian*, 7 January 1971).

This particular customer had set out to buy a Triumph Herald but had been told that there was a six-month waiting-list (a sale lost to British Leyland). Seeing a line of new Vivas and liking their looks he had asked about the price, had been taken on a trial drive (in one belonging to the showroom manager and driven by the salesman) and had eventually decided to trade in his Ford Cortina at an average level of settlement.

He paid cash for the balance of the price and took delivery of the car a few weeks later. This owner was not a long-distance driver and did not use his car every day, so that when the first fault occurred within a month (failure of thermostat causing over-heating) the vehicle had not done more than 500 miles. This repair was done by Henlys under guarantee, but that car was off the road for four days, including a weekend, when the unhappy owner was committed to driving a friend into the country. Car hire cost him £20.

At the beginning of December he took the car in for its free 1,000-mile check, after which according to his correspondence with the dealers it was worse than before. Early in the New Year he lost patience and sent a list of complaints to the managing director of Vauxhall, and to Henlys, addressing it to the salesman. The list had nine items: engine stalling on declutching; intermittent carburation; a broken quarter-light lock; broken fascia panel (this had been observed within days of taking possession but he had assumed that it would be repaired at the 1,000-mile check); faulty wipers; stiff gearbox; the passenger door seal adrift; the carpet adrift; and a general complaint that the paint and chrome were peeling at numerous points.

At this time the owner had not been given a Vauxhall warranty or he would have known that most of these defects were not covered. In his innocence he had thought that when he bought a car (all his previous purchases but the Cortina had been of secondhand cars checked by the Automobile Association) either it would work and be of a reasonable standard of finish or that the makers would put it right during the first year or 12,000 miles.

In his letter to the salesman he commented that 'For all the publicity and styling I think that the Viva (or this one at least) is poor value for money. I will certainly never buy another.' To the managing director of Vauxhall, who at that time was Mr David Hegland and from whom he did not receive a reply, he said, among other things, 'I am not a motor mechanic, only a motorist who drives because it is a convenient mode of transport—but not in this car, my first and conceivably my last Vauxhall.'

Henlys replied by return that their Service Manager would take the matter up, which he did by telephone, and in went the ill-fated car for the third time in just over four months. Vauxhall left it to their Owner Relations Manager, who passed the buck politely to Henlys while apologizing for 'your problems'. The phrase is striking in its implication that the affair was no direct concern of the manufacturing company.

The Viva was collected by the owner after a week and he found that only three of the nine defects had been remedied: the engine stall, the petrol feed, and the window lock. He pointed this out in a letter to the salesman, who again passed him on to the Service Manager. Simultaneously the owner wrote a letter to the Owner Relations Manager at Vauxhall pointing out that the Viva's five-inch ground clearance made it impossible for him to use an automatic multistorey car park near his place of work. He added that the car was still out of order, that he was dissatisfied with it and suggested a replacement.

Customer relations

The Owner Relations Manager's reply was a masterpiece and deserves lengthy quotation.

> I think our sales figures are a good yardstick to go by when arriving at a degree of popularity of the series HB Viva car, which as you know, is extremely good.

No one had yet mentioned popularity. And what did the manager consider good, the sales figures or the car? Certainly the now desperate owner was far from enthusiastic. The Owner Relations Manager went on:

> Whenever mass production is undertaken, there are bound to be cases similar to yours, and this is one of the reasons why we give a warranty for 12 months or 12,000 miles, and I would also like to point out that we, as a

Company, prefer to regard our warranty more from a moral than a legal point of view, and often assist with rectification work after the warranty expired, based on the merits of each individual case, and that very careful records are kept, of complaints received by owner's (*sic*) of our products.

That sentence is worth study by any aspiring marketeer, not for its literary merit, but for the implication, once again, that a faulty car is an inevitable by-product of the mass production system and that a proportion of unfortunate customers is 'bound' to get one. The Owner Relations Manager nevertheless followed up his apologia with 'I cannot accede to your request that we replace this car, and I do not think that you have any cause to think in these terms.' Considering that a car is the most expensive consumer durable that an individual can buy (excepting a house, which is intrinsically a different class of purchase) such a statement is ludicrous. If someone buys an unsatisfactory consumer product he is entitled to ask for a substitute and get it. What right has the company's representative to say that in his opinion the customer has no cause to believe this?

The sequel in this case was that Vauxhall's district service engineer was instructed to join the Henlys service team in examining the offending automobile. Meanwhile the car had broken down again and the owner, of necessity, had had to use the services of a local garage, which had changed the sparking plugs and cleaned and adjusted the points and adjusted the carburettor. Some of these were supposed to have been done, and one service at least in this group was alleged to have been done again at Henlys, which is another story.

In mid March 1969, the owner protested to Henlys at the cost to him of the car's being constantly out of service, adding that in his opinion the car was unfit for service when he took delivery, and hinting at his statutory rights under the Sale of Goods Act. The point was not taken up by either firm, but the owner received an invoice from Henlys for the last repair work, even though the car was still under warranty. He returned this invoice and demanded a copy of the manufacturer's terms, which he had not yet seen. He had not read the small print when he bought the car, that is, Henlys' conditions of sale, which said that they would supply a copy of the maker's warranty on request.

He was sent, not a copy of the complete warranty, which must be a lengthy document, but only photocopies of pages 4 and 6 of Section 7, headed 'Items not covered for the Warranty Period'. It was then that he learnt just how little of a car is covered by the manufacturer's guarantee. For example, under a sub-heading 'Body' there are nine separate groups of items not covered, including alignment of doors, bonnet and boot lid, all locks, and any fastenings throughout the car. No wonder he had received a bill. Obviously Henlys did not want to bear the cost of adjustments for which they could not be reimbursed by the maker. But why should the customer be made to pay for assembly line faults?

He pointed out to Henlys that, had he bought the car under a hire-purchase agreement and not paid cash, he would now refuse to continue payment and allow them to repossess the car, forfeiting whatever he had paid. But, it seems, a cash customer is in a weaker position than one buying on credit, in such circumstances. For the record, by this time the list of defects had been enlarged to include the petrol gauge, air filter, spark plugs, and an indicator warning light. The customer was beginning to wish that he had never heard of the Vauxhall Viva, let alone bought one.

It was by then the end of March, and the owner was unimpressed to hear that Vauxhall's District Inspector had been instructed to have a look at his car. He now wanted to get rid of the car and forget all about it. But he agreed to take it in once again for this inspection. To his astonished delight the inspector agreed with all his strictures and reported this to Luton, at which point Vauxhall hinted that they might bear the cost of the last repair work. Accordingly he wrote to the Owner Relations Manager requesting assurance that he would not have to pay for repairs under warranty.

He received a reply which contained no reference whatsoever to this request. In part the letter said:

Our engineer has reported that, in general, your vehicle is of a representative condition although a complete paint finish check could not be carried out.

On his road test he could find no difficulty with the gear change mechanism of your vehicle. What you may be confused with is the carburation flat spot. This would tend to cause the vehicle to miss on change over from slow running to progression.

I understand our engineer has agreed to change the offside vent and also to refinish the window surrounds and to change the passenger fresh air vent. It would have been far more beneficial if you could have met the engineer to discuss with him any problems that are causing concern.

It is interesting to notice the mild rebuke that the customer was unable to be present at the inspection, and the absence of any reference to compensation or the meeting of the costs of these endless inspections and repairs. The last straw for this owner was the jamming down of the driving window during a long journey in rain. Arriving at his destination wet through he took his car in for repair and was rather upset when the mechanic who got the window mechanism working again laughed at the poor quality of the 'refinish' on the window surrounds. He decided to get rid of the car there and then.

He wrote to this effect to Vauxhall, but never received any reply. Henlys kept up correspondence for a few more weeks, mainly because the owner refused to pay a bill for the last set of repairs. In July, about two months after the customer had sold his car, Henlys conceded the disputed amount, and the affair could be considered closed, except for the fact that this customer was a journalist and managed to publish an article recounting the main points that have been given here. Neither firm responded to this move, evidently preferring to let the whole business blow over.

Car defects

However, this is not an isolated instance of offhand and even arrogant treatment of customers by the motor manufacturing industry. There followed in the press several articles by dissatisfied journalists, one of them a motoring correspondent. Then, in January 1970, the Consumers' Association published in *Which?* their analysis of the 30,000 questionnaires returned by their members who had been asked detailed and searching queries about the cars they owned.

Fig. 1.1, reproduced with permission of Consumers' Association, shows the position of Vauxhall in the Time Off Road league table. It shows a consistently poor record. The proportion of Vauxhalls owned and off the road for a week or more in 1969 was about 28 per cent, which matches the individual owner's experience, as recounted above, closely enough to be significant. Of course, the motor car manufacturers denounced the Consumers' Association survey as unscientific, biased, and improperly conducted. They were particularly outraged that foreign cars did comparatively well, notably Volkswagen and Volvo. During the controversy in early January 1970

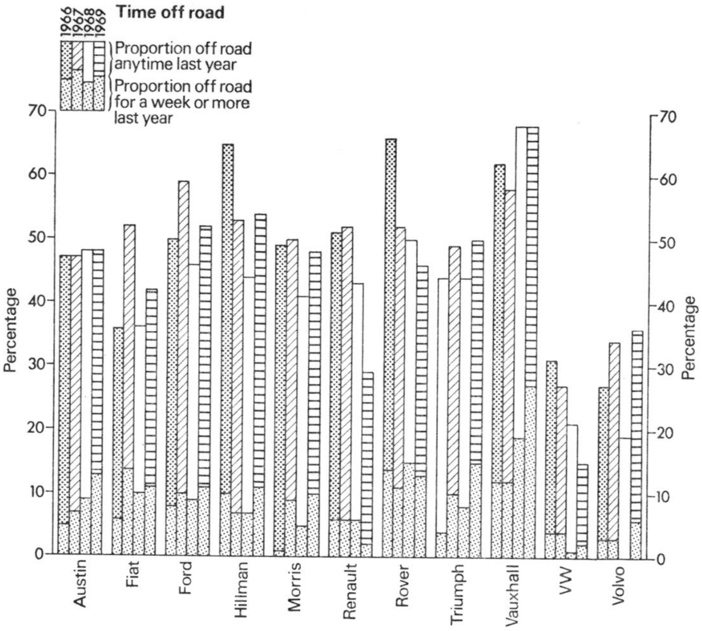

Fig. 1.1. Out of action

Looking at the proportion of each make which was never off the road for mechanical repair last year gives the following results for cars bought in:

1966. Volkswagen and Volvo significantly better than Hillman, Rover, and Vauxhall.

1967. Volkswagen significantly better than all except Volvo.

1968. Volkswagen and Volvo significantly better than all except Fiat. Vauxhall significantly worse than the other ten.

1969. Volkswagen significantly better than the other ten. Renault significantly better than all others except Fiat and Volvo. Vauxhall significantly worse than the other ten.

We also looked at the reliability of other makes for which we had smaller samples—usually cars owned by between 50 and 500 members.

The following makes seemed better than average: BMW, Daf, Mercedes, Peugeot, and (when bought new) NSU, Saab, and Simca.

These makes seemed about average: Alfa Romeo, Auto-Union, Citroen, Daimler, Humber, MG, Reliant, Riley, Singer, Vanden Plas, Wolseley.

These makes seemed worse than average: Jaguar, Lotus, and (when bought used) Citroen, Humber, Reliant, and Riley.

Among Japanese cars, all very young, with tiny samples, Honda did poorly, Datsun and Toyota well.

With the exceptions of Volvo (which remained very good) and Jaguar and Vauxhall (which became no worse), second-hand cars of each make spent more time off the road than new ones.

not a word was uttered by the car makers that suggested they were in the least bit interested in the reactions of 30,000 customers.

Coincidentally there was a study of British cars in comparison with foreign makes, imports of which had been increasing markedly, in the quarterly magazine of the Automobile Association, *Drive*. The British cars which had suffered most heavily from replacement by foreign makes were the Rover and Triumph 2000, the main reasons given being slow delivery (which was the reason why the Viva buyer switched from a Triumph Herald). But the Vauxhall series had also suffered some substitution by Fiat and Renault, and here the two chief reasons were poor finish and 'Too costly/not good value', with unreliability as a third reason. The *Drive* sample was small, only thirty-two Vauxhall owners being involved, but there was no comparable outcry from the industry such as had greeted the *Which?* report.

What emerges from this one account of how a customer was treated by a car maker hardly needs to be spelled out. On the general evidence, Vauxhall products do not give satisfaction in comparison with their competitors. Fig. 1.2, also reproduced from *Which?*, shows the proportion of vehicles breaking down on journeys over the years 1966–9, the black areas indicating two or more breakdowns. Again Vauxhall out-tops all the rest by a considerable margin.

But the Owner Relations Manager at Luton seemed to take the view that the faulty vehicle sold to the customer with whom he was in correspondence for several months was both 'representative' of the Luton assembly line output, and therefore presumably 'normal', and also belonged to a 'popular' series. Here emerges the short-term and long-term relationship in marketing a complex product like an automobile. Given an attractive appearance, such as the Viva undoubtedly had, for the purpose of exhibition and illustration, plus a vigorous launch and a good reception from the motoring correspondents (a notoriously uncritical group), allied to an advertising appropriation sufficient to make the influential dealers happy, and not too high a price, there would be bound to be a good take off. Even the ill-fated Edsel began fairly well, according to the account by John Brooks. Coupled with these factors was the additional advantage that the Viva was filling a gap in the popular car range, in some opinions anyway.

By all accounts, in the long run the car turned out to be less than reliable and disillusion began to affect customers at about the same

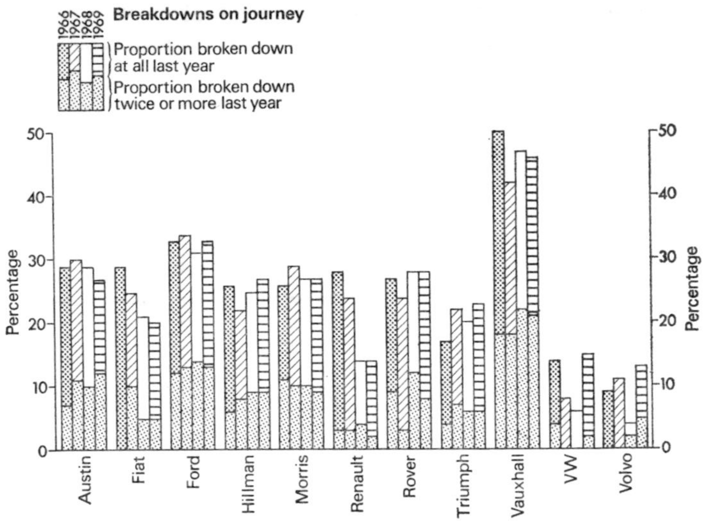

Fig. 1.2. Breakdowns

Looking at the proportion of each make which *never* broke down last year, depending on the year they were bought, shows:

1966. Volkswagen and Volvo significantly better than Ford or Vauxhall. Vauxhall significantly worse than Austin, Morris, and Triumph.

1967. Volkswagen and Volvo significantly better than Ford or Vauxhall. Volkswagen also significantly better than Austin or Morris. Vauxhall significantly worse than Hillman or Triumph.

1968. Volkswagen and Volvo significantly better than all but Renault. Renault and Triumph significantly better than Austin, Ford, or Vauxhall. Vauxhall significantly worse than the other ten.

1969. Renault, Volkswagen, and Volvo significantly better than Ford or Vauxhall. Renault and Volkswagen also significantly better than Morris and Rover. Renault also significantly better than Austin and Hillman. Vauxhall significantly worse than the other ten.

Among other cars, Auto-Union, BMW, Daf, Mercedes, Puegeot, Saab, and (when bought new) Daimler and Simca seemed better than average.

Alfa Romeo, Citroen, Humber, Jaguar, MG, NSU, Singer, Sunbeam, Vanden Plas, and Wolseley seemed above average.

Lotus, Reliant, and Riley seemed worse than average.

Japanese cars did quite well. Datsun and Toyota better than Honda.

Cars bought second-hand were generally a little worse than the equivalent new cars. On average, the drop was bigger for foreign cars than for British ones, though foreign cars in general were still significantly less likely to break down than British ones. Second-hand Vauxhalls did a little better than new ones.

time that the two rivals began to enter the market. Whether Vauxhall could have withstood this competition had the Viva been all that its purchasers hoped we cannot say. But looking at the sad saga of the company's declining fortunes it seems to be part of an all-round management failure (see for example, 'Why the quiet years ended at Luton', *The Times*, 11 September 1970).

Did the Owner Relations Manager do all that he could, in the circumstances, to satisfy an increasingly dissatisfied customer? From the correspondence alone it would not appear that he did. He would be in a better position than the admittedly non-technical car owner to understand the whole problem. For example, he said in one letter that careful records were kept of complaints. It is unlikely that the proportion would be so different from that in the *Which?* sample as to merit the complacency exhibited by the manager in the letter referring to the satisfactory sales figures. The impression is left with the reader of these extracts from the correspondence that to this manager and perhaps to this firm the complaining customer is a nuisance.

A wiser attitude, from the long-term marketing point of view, would be to regard the dissatisfied (and the satisfied) customer as 'feedback', to be taken into account and used to improve performance. Unfortunately satisfied customers rarely communicate their approval ('unsolicited testimonials' belong to the category of marketing mythology), but this fact is well known and should not be allowed to generate the feeling that the complainers are fusspots and cranks. If and when a manufacturing company cannot absorb and make use of criticism from the people whose purchases provide its profits, it is heading for trouble.

There is an interesting piece of corroboration of this Vauxhall story in Graham Turner's paperback *Cars* (in the Zenith Industry and People series, 1965). In the section 'A car is made' he describes the design process and the preparation for production of the Viva at Luton. He describes how the company, in common with other mass producers of cars, passes directly from the hand-made prototype to line production. He goes on: 'However accurately the designer may have worked, this can clearly lead to enormous problems. Sometimes parts simply do not fit.' The result is that numbers of models go to the dealers in a faulty condition, even with rain leaks from ill-fitting panels. Turner comments: 'What this means very simply is that the public pays for unsatisfactory proving—and some of the industry's top engineers admit it.'

A letter in *The Times* on 13 January 1971 put the faultiness of cars down to the use of the management technique called 'value analysis' which is a fancy new name for cost reduction. Every product is scrutinized for cheap material or part substitutes. 'Particularly fruitful ground for this technique is inspection, which adds nothing to the value of a good product but on faulty ones can save the cost difference between a production line remedy and a subsequent repair.'

If the repair cost can be passed on to the dealer, or even to the customer (who pays is evidently a matter of indifference to the maker just as long as he can keep the percentage of returned cars down to 10 per cent or below), it is probably worthwhile to drop or at least reduce inspection. Complaints from abroad cost more to handle so export models are more carefully inspected, which is the reason for a British customer finding chalked on the chassis of his defective car 'Not fit for export'.

The Times correspondent surmised that too few customers actually complain to the makers. But what good did it do our customer who bought a Viva? Very little in the end. Graham Turner, in his earlier book *The Car Makers* (Eyre & Spottiswoode, 1963), has a chapter entitled 'Why the quality of our cars suffers'. In it he gives in some detail an account of the hit and miss methods of assembly line car production, and makes a prophetic comment on the losing battle with the Continental car makers. The percentage of the British home market captured by foreign makes has doubled from 8 in 1968 to an estimated 16 in 1971, and is now about 27 per cent, and a prime reason is quality and reliability. ('Home truths on car imports', *The Times*, 12 April 1973.)

Yet the British car makers, or some of them, tend to take the attitude that they cannot improve reliability without raising prices. An appendix to *The Car Makers* gives a manufacturer's reply to Turner's strictures on skimped work and touching-up. First, this manager surmised that Graham Turner had met mainly shopfloor 'grumblers' and similar troublemakers. Why else did not the chapter contain comments on good quality control? Then he accused the writer of confusing quality control with inspection, passing on to assert that 'warranty costs' were low enough to show that few cars were produced with defects (yet most production line defects are not covered by guarantee). Finally, he made a grandiose statement about the superiority of British cars to foreign, without producing any statistics such as import figures to back it up.

The Research Institute for Consumer Affairs reported in 1965, in *Car Defects*, that of a sample of 52 cars tested every one had at least one visible defect, and the average was 17. Rain leaks were found in 71 per cent, wheel imbalance in 65 per cent, incorrect valve clearances in 62 per cent and engine faults in 42 per cent. The total number of defects found in the 52 cars was 1,396, an average of 27 per car. At Vauxhall, asking about pre-delivery inspections, they discovered that only about 65 per cent of PDI reports are returned, although it was assumed that 90 per cent of the PDIs had been done. The company had set up a Reliability Division in 1961 and to RICA the company gave 'the impression of being extremely conscious of quality', operating a points system for faults. Each car began with 100 points and lost a certain number for each defect according to its seriousness. If the figure fell below 95 a special inspection had to be undertaken. That year they claimed an average score of 96·8.

That percentage would have been for 1964. The two *Which?* tables begin in 1966 and indicate a sharp decline in car reliability in the case of Vauxhall in particular. Only the company really knows the explanation for such an increasingly poor record. But Vauxhall is by no means alone in the motor industry in claiming that outside criticism is not only at variance with its own experience but also based on faulty data collection and reasoning.

Yet in 1968 the Swedish Government's car-testing agency placed British cars at the bottom of its ranking of foreign cars for reliability. (They shared this honour with the Russians. The only Moskvich the author has ever driven literally fell to pieces during a fortnight's hire in Bulgaria.) A year earlier *Drive* had looked at reliability and placed imported cars top with nearly 80 per cent fault free. (Although they represented a mere 4 per cent of the sample of about 300 cars. Could this just be luck?) In that test the low scorer was the Ford Anglia with around 17 per cent fault free, and the runners up (or down) were the Rootes Imp and the Vauxhall Viva with the Viva having about 28 per cent fault free and the Imp 29.

The evidence that British cars have deteriorated in quality, in the sense that they are delivered with multiple defects in increasing numbers (if mass produced) is overwhelming. The manufacturers stoutly if not stubbornly deny it. But the British public, equally stubborn in its loyalty to the industry (it still offends some Britons to find German or Japanese or even American cars being preferred) is now giving way and buying foreign. There must be a reason, perhaps more than one. In this chapter we have attempted to suggest an important one. But the implicit message is that this need not have happened if the British motor industry had listened to its customers and their advisers, notably the Automobile Association and the Consumers' Association Car Test Unit. Neither of these is happy to report adversely on their own country's car engineering. It does seem as if the car makers have been using the British market as a 'sink' instead of a 'source', a shortsighted policy in view of the United Kingdom's importance as a home base.

According to Dr R. M. Belbin's *Quality Calamities and their Managment Implications* (BIM, 1970) the car industry is outstanding for its contribution to his collection of 'calamities', usually the more costly examples. In general, he also points out that some manufacturers do not even know the use to which their product will be put. The car industry has no such excuse.

Footnote to Case 1. In April 1973 it was reported that the Vauxhall Firenza (more or less the Viva under another name) would no longer be exported to Canada, after nationwide protests from the Association of Dissatisfied Firenza Owners—about 1,500 strong—who staged a 30-mile protest cavalcade to General Motors' HQ in Ontario. *Campaign*, 27 April 1973.

CASE

2 *The appliance nobody wanted*

It seems that the British like washing up, or perhaps they do not dislike it enough to invest in a machine to wash the dishes for them. The annual market for dishwashers in Britain was stuck for years at 30,000 a year and in 1972 was about 70,000 (including imports.) In the United States about two million machines are sold each year. In West Germany about half a million were bought in 1969. Even in Italy sales have reached 250,000 a year.

What reasons can seriously be offered for this resistance to the dishwasher? Commonly five are offered. Dishwashers are too expensive, but they are cheaper than many other appliances which have six-figure annual sales. There is no room for them in the average kitchen but the clothes washing machine also had to overcome this objection, and succeeded. They will not wash everything, but neither will a clothes washer, yet women tolerate this. They do not work properly. Some do, some do not, but you could say the same of any electrical appliance. They damage delicate crockery and glass. But a washing machine will damage delicate items of clothing. These are the dishwasher manufacturers' stock answers to the consumers' stock objections, and they have been arguing thus for well over a d cade without apparent effect.

To understand this particular marketing problem better it is instructive to look at the experience of the late Sir Charles Colston and his son Michael, the present chairman and managing director of Colston Appliances Ltd. They formed the company in 1958 about a year after Sir Charles had resigned from Hoover, of which he had been managing director for thirty-seven years. His reasons for leaving that company were purely personal and quite unconnected with his eventual decision to launch a British-designed dishwasher (the first, as it happened), although he was under an obligation not to compete with his former company, his lifetime's experience was in domestic appliances and a dishwasher was about the only major household gadget that Hoover did not make at that time.

It seems, in the cant phrase, that the Colstons were 'ahead of their time', which is a backhanded compliment to all innovators. They had calculated on reaching 'a substantial level of sales' by 1960, within two years of launching their first design, but twelve years later the market not only showed no sign of expansion but became crowded with competitors, which is a curious paradox. When *Which?* the monthly journal of the Consumers' Association, surveyed dishwashers for the first time in December 1960, there were six makes available and the ownership figure was less than one in two hundred households compared with one in sixteen in the United States. Today there is a score of makes of dishwasher on the British market, including importers, and the ownership percentage is just over one (1·2 is the estimate), with annual sales stuck at about 70,000. Colston's three models probably hold the largest single percentage (or at least are in the top bracket) but it hardly constitutes 'brand leadership in a mass market', which was the company's original ambition.

Sir Charles himself evidently believed that one factor in the reluctance of the British housewife (or her husband) to invest in a dishwasher was the highly critical *Which?* report. Although it did put forward a preference for three of the makes, the report was larded with depressing comments about the hazards of the machines: that spoons might fall into the water impeller and break its blades, or be flung about inside and smash plates, that machines did not switch off at the end of the washing cycle and that they overflowed. The general conclusion was that dishwashers were not yet 'the equal of a good, conscientious hand-washer'. This was a reference to the quality of the washing rather than to the time it took. But the detailed comments looked as if they might dissuade potential buyers much more certainly than the summing up.

According to Mr Michael Colston's own recollection of the impact of the *Which?* article, weekly sales dropped almost immediately by about 15 per cent, but within six months of publication, that is by the summer of 1961, had climbed back to normal. Nevertheless, Sir Charles issued a counter-statement to the press about the Consumers' Association report and thereafter kept up a fairly steady campaign. In October 1965, *Which?* had a second look at dishwashers, which were still lagging in the appliance ownership tables (indeed, they were too small to include), and reported favourably on their reliability and servicing, while commenting on their high price. The conclusion this time was that people who did not like washing up might find the investment worth while. The report added that most of the Consumers' Association members polled on this question had replied that they did not find the task 'onerous'. The Best Buy was the Colston Mark IV.

If the early criticisms of *Which?* had retarded Colston sales, which apparently they did but only temporarily, it might be expected that this recommendation should have had the opposite effect, but Mr Colston does not recollect any noticeable peak in sales thereafter. Even had there been, it is equally logical to conclude that sales would have levelled off as before.

Stagnant market

What is much more significant is the stagnation not only of Colston sales over the past twelve years but of the whole dishwasher market, and to explain this phenomenon it is necessary to look a little deeper than simple 'customer resistance' fortified, perhaps, by the initial opposition of *Which?* Indeed, when the Colston dishwasher was launched in 1958 it received a favourable press and gave a fillip to the dishwasher market in general. Since when there have been numerous efforts in the form of public relations campaigns to get the market 'off the ground'.

For example, the British Electrical and Allied Manufacturers' Association, now replaced for the appliance makers by the Association of Manufacturers of Domestic Electrical Appliances, ran the Dishwasher Information Service on a small budget provided by the United Kingdom based manufacturers. It issued a bulletin for press and retailers called *Dishwasher News* and, in 1968, staged a 'teach-in' on dishwashers to attract more attention still from the communications media. None of this effort appears to have done more for the market than give it temporary boosts. There does not seem to have been any significant long-term shift in demand.

It is never wise to offer cut and dried explanations of such situations, but as far as the British experience goes there is an interesting correlation to be found in the growth of ownership of at least three large items of domestic equipment during the period 1955–60, which covers the emergence of the dishwasher and the apparently abortive attempts at its diffusion among households. The washing machine for clothes, the refrigerator, and the television set all show dramatic growth in the late 1950s and early to middle 1960s. The following table summarizes the 1961–9 developments over a range of appliances, all of which must have made inroads into the disposable incomes of households, leaving little scope for spending on an appliance which seems to have been regarded as marginal by a sample of consumers.

Table 2.1. *Ownership of domestic appliances (percentage of households).*

	1961	*1969*
Washing machines	41	64
Refrigerators	23	54
Water heaters	36	56
Electric blankets	19	50
Vacuum cleaners	75	83
Food mixers	3	22

The contrasts are even more dramatic if the percentages are taken back to the 1950s, when, for example, refrigerator ownership was as little as 5 per cent. It must also be remembered that these were years when motor-car ownership was also growing steeply, and there was the beginning of a campaign to sell small-bore central heating systems. Television set ownership and rental may be gauged from the issue of licences which, during the decade 1960–70, rose from about ten million to seventeen million, and this does not take into account the unlicensed sets that were probably installed.

Later in the period further temptations were placed in the way of families: the automatic washing machine, colour television, packaged holidays (which reveal a steep growth curve in the relevant period), and unexpectedly after the initial slow growth of refrigerator sales, the deep freeze cabinet. The inference that may be drawn from comparing these figures with the contemporaneous data in the annual *Family Income and Expenditure Blue Book* is that 1955–65 and thereafter was a period of increasing affluence in the A, B, and C1 income groups: the upper middle and middle classes and the 'upper working class', if such loose terminology is still permissible. At the same time it was also a period during which this affluence could be exerted in purchasing an increasing range of possessions, all of which would be in competition for the disposable income available after unavoidable, essential disbursements had been made. Furthermore, it was a period when hire purchase and credit sales were on the increase to the extent that they became sufficiently important to be used as economic regulators in pursuit of the so-called 'stop-go' policies of the time.

Any businessman who was keeping an eye on economic trends at that time would have realized that there were rich opportunities in the growth of disposable family income, and would act accordingly, as Sir Charles Colston did. He had a personal recollection of the slow take-off of the vacuum cleaner in Britain. First introduced by Hoover in 1919, it was 1936 before sales had reached a really profitable level. What lay behind this particular sluggishness is not relevant to this case-history, no doubt the existence of a large and low-paid army of domestic servants had something to do with it, but it seems to have coloured Sir Charles's thinking, in that he was not shocked by the early setback, merely disappointed.

It is interesting, however, to study briefly what the members of the Consumers' Association were thinking in 1965, according to the October issue of *Which?*

It is clear from our members' experience [said the report], that the reliability and servicing of dishwashers is no longer a special problem.

This time our members did not show the disappointment with washing performance that they sometimes expressed in 1963. And in our tests we found that very few things were left with dirty food traces: with the best machine (the Colston Mark IV) this was not a problem at all.

Some people don't find washing up particularly onerous; for them paying a lot of money for a dishwasher would not be worth while. But a lot of people do find it a burden, and would be prepared to pay a lot of money for an effective method of avoiding it. If you are one of these, we think you would not be disappointed in the best of the dishwashers we have tested this time.

The phrase 'a lot of money' occurs twice, suggesting that dishwashers are in some way more expensive than other appliances of similar size and technical content. They are not, although the price range is wide, varying from about £50 to about £250 in 1968. No wonder that Sir Charles continued to be mildly irritated by the *Which?* reports even after they had not only revised their general opinion of dishwashers but had selected his own machine as Best Buy. The general tone of the 1965 report reflects the marginal view that people seemed to persist in talking of the dishwasher as a possession. And by all accounts this view still persists in Britain.

An interesting aspect of the dishwasher story is the interest taken in this Cinderella of appliances by the Consumers' Association. They published reports in 1960, 1965, and 1968 as well as short comments and supplementary reports on single makes in intervening years. Over-all, however, the influence of *Which?* on the dishwasher market seems to have been negligible either way. The determining influences, which appear to have been negative, must be traced elsewhere, and the most that can be said is that, in Britain at least, the dishwasher had not been accorded a high enough priority in the variety of options open to the affluent household.

Sir Charles was fortunate in that he did not put all his eggs in the one basket. He had acquired a versatile engineering business and, since the expiry of his Hoover covenant, it had been possible for it to enter the appliance field over a broader front. The dishwasher is not such an important segment of Colston Appliances business that to drop it would be a disaster, although Michael Colston has no intention of doing that.

The nub of this case-history is simply that a general prediction of rising real incomes, and even of increasing disposable incomes, is insufficient by itself to act as a decisive indicator in a new marketing situation. The Colstons did go to the trouble of having a market research survey done. The results did not please them, because they were negative, and they decided to go ahead anyway, on the basis of hunch. Hunch is not necessarily a bad thing, but in this particular case it would have been salutary to take a look at the environmental trends as well. Today the company is well aware that a large part of its competition lies with other appliances and not simply with competing brands.

A token of this understanding is the setting up of the Dishwasher Development Council, under the auspices of AMDEA, but with an adequate budget and, contrary to some feelings in the industry, with the inclusion of importers. The idea, then, is to propagate the general idea of dishwasher ownership as a good and desirable thing. It is a move that was made with resounding success by the refrigerator manufacturers in the mid 1950s when, exasperated by slow build-up of their market, they set up the Domestic Refrigerator Development Committee, with the intention of educating British families in the all-year-round usefulness of the appliance, even in a north European climate.

It would be foolish to ascribe the subsequent growth of refrigerator ownership in Britain entirely, or perhaps at all, to the work of that committee. All that we can safely say is that after its establishment ownership grew by an order of ten in just over a decade. It may be that the Dishwasher Development Council will be able to do the same for what we used to call the washing-up machine. Time will tell as usual.

CASE

3 *Luck of the Irish*

The Irish Sugar Company was founded in 1933 on similar lines to the British Sugar Corporation, a government-financed and supported organization refining and marketing beet sugar. In its forty years of existence it has diversified into other food-processing activities using since 1960 a wholly owned subsidiary called Erin Foods Ltd.

Erin Foods was founded as part of the Irish Government's economic expansion programme promulgated in 1958, with the avowed object of developing export markets. Erin's functions were to procure vegetables grown under contract, process them in various ways (drying, canning, and freezing), to procure and process fish and meat products as well, to develop packet soups and 'instant meals' and 'to sell all these products in Ireland and abroad'.

This ambitious plan rested partly on the conviction that Irish agriculture could produce the raw materials at competitive costs and yet maintain high quality, and that there would be more use of labour in the market-garden sector of farming than in livestock husbandry. It did necessitate an educational programme, organized by the ISC's agricultural advisory service, because the success of food processing depends on the quality of the raw materials, especially with drying, which was Erin Foods' dominant preoccupation. There were some canning operations, but the bias towards dehydration by air drying was evident, with plants at Carlow, Mallow, Tuam (potato flakes), and at least three other centres.

It was at Mallow that the first freeze-drying plant was put up in 1960 and opened in May 1961. It was built by Vickers at a total cost estimated to be £250,000, the original design being derived from the Ministry of Agriculture's installation at the Torry Research Station near Aberdeen, where work on what was then called accelerated freeze-drying had been going on since 1951. Initially work at the experimental factory was based on vacuum contact dehydration as developed by the A/S Atlas company of Copenhagen, which had taken out British patents in 1948.

There were numerous modifications to the Atlas system and in 1958 AFD, or rather the apparatus and its design, were patented by the National Research Development Corporation on behalf of the inventors, J. M. Dalgleish and H. P. Thompson. Until the registration of this patent the AFD work had been done in comparative secrecy as it was looked upon as a defence development, for the preservation, storage, and transport of food in time of war. The AFD process transforms fresh food, by first freezing it and then under pressure vaporizing the ice, into a state where it is lighter in weight by the amount of moisture it has lost, may be stored without temperature control but requires to be kept dry, and has a shelf life estimated in years rather than months.

It is not difficult to grasp why some commercial companies saw interesting and possibly profitable advantages in this new if untried preservation method. During the early stages of the work Unilever had become involved and eventually, when the Ministry decided to withdraw from the exercise, handed over the experimental factory to that company. Eventually it was the Batchelors subsidiary of the group, taken over in 1943, which was given the job of applying the process and marketing the products.

There is a great deal more to the complex history of freeze-drying than can possibly be covered in this brief chapter, which is intended to focus upon the reasons for Erin Foods' initial failure in this new sector of food processing. As far as the technology of AFD was concerned the company began with a relative disadvantage, having not had the first-hand knowledge acquired by the Unilever team which had been attached to the Ministry of Food during the Second World War and some of whom continued to work with the Torry researchers after the war.

As far as can reliably be ascertained, a former general manager of ISC, Lt-Gen. M. J. Costello, was the initiator of the venture, which had its origins in the need to maintain the level of employment in Irish agriculture, threatened by falling land use as a result of higher yields per acre, and a fact-finding visit of the general's to Torry, when by accident he met two senior engineers from Vickers. Vickers had set up a food-processing division as early as 1958 to design and market AFD equipment. The sale to ISC of £100,000 worth of hardware in 1960–1 was almost a third of the company's total business during 1960–3. By 1966 they realized that this branch of their business was not paying and sold it to the French firm Socaltra in 1967.

In practice, AFD turned out to be a high-cost operation, compared with other processes, as Table 3.1 shows. The table is a little mis-

Table 3.1.

	Capital cost	*Running cost*
Canning	100	100
Air drying	150	128
Freezing	150	136
AFD	500	320

Index numbers based on canning costs = 100.

leading because of the batch process used in AFD, which has proved difficult to make continuous. Canning and air-drying are continuous processes and freezing is rapidly converting to flow systems. But the cost disadvantage certainly applied to the plant at Mallow operated by Erin Foods, and this was not fully appreciated at the outset. To make the most economical use of such high-cost plant a high utilization rate is necessary, even a shift system round the clock if possible. For this a large and steady sale is essential and Erin Foods did not obtain a sufficient market share to make this achievable.

International competition

They were, of course, facing among others three large international competitors: Unilever, through Batchelors and Bird's Eye; Corn Products, through Knorr; and Nestlé, through Maggi. Apart from an insufficiently clear realization of the competition they were taking on in the British food market, it is also evident that Erin Foods had failed to think on general lines. Their AFD products were not just competing with other dried foods but with all processed foods. This typical attack of marketing myopia may explain why they overlooked a trend that was progressively narrowing the market for dried foods.

Traditionally the British housewife, unlike the American housewife, has managed without a cold store, an icebox, or a refrigerator. At one time, before the development of apartment blocks, middle-class families in Britain had houses with larders or pantries. Sometimes an outside 'meat safe' was used. Summertime was a particular problem for such families, with the danger of contamination by flies and the difficulty of protecting milk and cream from premature souring. Hardware shops used to sell porous earthenware butter-dishes with glass linings in which butter could be kept without melting, and there were earthenware covers for milk bottles which could be damped and could cool the milk by evaporation.

As late as 1956 the Domestic Refrigerator Development Committee of the British Refrigeration Association estimated refrigerator ownership in Britain as no more than 7 per cent of households. DORDEC was set up to promote the sales of these appliances on behalf of the manufacturers, and began a public relations campaign in 1956–7, aimed at educating the public away from its apparent belief that refrigerators are only of use in the summer. Sales were sharply seasonal, peaking in the warmer weather, and the annual market was no more than 200,000 units on average.

The limited ownership of refrigerated food stores was also a limiting factor in the sales of frozen foods. Although people without refrigerators did buy frozen foods, they had to eat them almost immediately and could not store them. As the ownership of refrigerators grew to 22 per cent in 1960, 40 per cent in 1965, and 58 per cent in 1969 so the market for frozen foods grew. According to figures derived by A. C. Nielsen from grocers' returns alone the sale of frozen peas went up from an annual £11 million (round figures) to over £17 million between 1965 and 1968, and of other frozen vegetables from £7½ million to over £14 million in the same period. Frozen fish in all forms had reached nearly £20 million in 1965 and nearly £28 million by 1968, with frozen meat at £16 million in that year.

The same source shows that sales of air-dried peas were static, even declining, and that various canned products, especially canned peas, were also sluggish, exceptions being baked beans and canned meat of various kinds. AFD foods held such a slight percentage of the processed foods market that they were not taken into account in these calculations. The correlation between refrigerator ownership and the increased popularity of frozen foods has, as far as I know, not been statistically confirmed, but that there has been coincidental growth cannot be denied. Anyone entering the processed food market in the 1960s, as Erin Foods did, would have been well advised to scrutinize all the trends associated with a particular process and its future before plumping for it. The 'relevance matrix' (Table 3.2) suggests how it might have been done.

Table 3.2. *A 'relevance matrix' for AFD foods.*

Alternative processes	None (fresh)	Canning	Air drying	Freezing	Smoking	Bottling, pickling
AFD substitution probability	Some	Some	Complete (?)	Some	None	None
Disadvantages of alternatives	Home storage Shelf life	Bulk weight	Reconstitution Flavour	Cost, cold storage in home and shops	Not relevant	Not relevant

To this 'array' could be added irradiation, but it is hardly of any importance as an alternative process now, and certainly was not when Erin Foods began using AFD.

The main opportunity shows up under air-drying, the process to which Batchelors reverted when they determined the high running cost of freeze-drying. Serious competitors with small substitution opportunities are: fresh foods, with their obvious disadvantages, including frequent purchases because of lack of adequate home storage facilities (refrigerator ownership in 1960 when Mallow went on stream was 22 per cent, leaving quite a gap, but it had doubled since 1958, which was worth noting): canned foods, well entrenched and familiar; frozen foods, just getting into their stride and riding on the back of the growth of refrigerator ownership; and air-drying. This last, with its recent history of wartime and post-war dehydration with all the connotations of austerity and food shortage that it conjures up, was an obvious opportunity. However, it had a cost advantage, and the technology had been much improved to make for better flavour and easier reconstitution.

A similar relevance array could then have been made to show possible outlets other than in processing agricultural or fishery products for retail distribution (a detailed display of foods to be treated would also display the limitations and opportunities of the technique). While freeze-drying has not been a great success in solid food processing for the retail market, it has been used more widely in supplying caterers, because of the labour-saving element, which offsets the cost, and because of ease of storage and length of shelf life. In addition the processing of liquids, 'instant' coffee, soups, fruit drinks, and lately tea, has shown itself to be highly successful in both outlets, a point which would not emerge from the first relevance matrix. It is not, therefore, just the rival processes at which one must look but the whole food and drink processing industry and its outlets.

The relevance matrix thus becomes a mnemonic, a reminder, that in embarking upon the use of a new technique there are more considerations than simply those of investment cost and payback, training of operational staff, marketing, and distribution, but also that there are other techniques available and in use by potential competitors.

There were other handicaps under which Erin Foods laboured, apart from lack of awareness of the competitive build-up in the United Kingdom market. Compared with the brand leaders theirs was an unknown name. The importance of having a 'household name' is brought out by the fact that after Erin Foods reached a joint marketing agreement with H. J. Heinz in April 1967, and Heinz-Erin was formed as a joint venture, sales went up from an annual £3 million in 1967–8 to £5,400,000 in 1968–9. Some at least of this big jump must have been due to association with the famous 57 varieties and its well-known label, as well as to better distribution and larger marketing facilities than Erin Foods had been able to afford on its own.

A large part of the losses of the new company in the years 1963–6, when they were trying to establish themselves in the British market, may be attributed to marketing costs. Accumulated losses during these three difficult years amounted to nearly £5 million. Erin Foods put a lot of effort into getting as wide a distribution for their products as possible. Their packet soups had a 22 per cent distribution, the annual market then, 1966, being calculated at £67 million, but achieved only 2·1 per cent market share. The same scale of response was true of their quick-dried peas, 11 per cent distribution and 3·8 per cent market share, and instant meals, 9 per cent distribution with 1·2 per cent market share. On the catering side a 3 per cent share was recorded. Consumer acceptance seemed to be the missing factor.

A detail of presentation reinforces the judgement that it was the individual consumer's response that had been overlooked by the marketing men of Erin. In the design of some of the packets in which the products appeared in the British shops, a facsimile rubber stamp or stencil of the mysterious letters AFD was superimposed on the wrappers. According to the recollections of those involved even shop assistants were unaware of the meaning of these initials. And where they were, if they did say 'accelerated freeze-dried', could not explain precisely what that meant. Usually they said it was a kind of dehydration, which was loosely true, and this put off all those shoppers who remembered the dehydrated foods of the war and immediate post-war years.

When Batchelors launched their range of instant meals under the Vesta brand, they eventually refrained from making any mention of the process used. In any case AFD was used for only a small proportion of the contents of these packages. After the Heinz-Erin agreement all existing products were withdrawn and a new jointly branded range was launched with the emphasis, not on process technology, but on quality: the Heinz-Erin Seal of Good Food.

Looking back on the first phase of the Erin Foods story, one may observe that at first general management had confused two objectives: the need to assist the solution of the agricultural unemployment problem in Ireland, and the need to make a profit. The consequence was that they concentrated on the production angle to the detriment of the marketing, although they went through all the routine marketing exercises they failed to see the end-products as the customer inevitably would: something new and a little mysterious but with no discernible advantages over existing brands. The USP was presented mysteriously as AFD, and in any case had lost much of its point by the mid 1960s. Only in 1966 did the company go to Arthur D. Little to find out where it had gone wrong and how to get matters right. Up to that time they had not systematically studied either the markets they were after nor the constituent individuals with the spending power.

Finally, they had tended to put all their financial eggs in one process basket, AFD, instead of considering a spread of processes of a more balanced kind. And they had chosen the most costly and therefore the most committing process in terms of market share needed to make it pay, launching it on rather too large a scale, leaving no scope for test marketing or pilot scale operation. The initial failure was not just the penalty of being pioneers. After all, the real British pioneers had been Unilever.

The Unilever researchers soon became aware of the high production costs involved in AFD and realized that it could only pay for itself if used on high value food products such as meat and fish. Today the only 'pure' freeze-dried product from Batchelors is the prawns used in the Vesta packs. Their big success, Surprise peas, is air-dried. A glance back at the table of cost indices shows the enormous cost difference between the two processes. By opting for the cheaper technology for a familiar product with a high sale Batchelors innovated successfully. But the decision to drop AFD for all product lines but one, after a high initial investment, must have been a hard one.

CASE

4 *The death of* London Life

Consumer product innovation is generally of the better mousetrap kind, such as a smaller portable radio, a cheaper washing machine, or a better carpet sweeper. The first wireless set (the valveless crystal set with its delicate 'cat's whisker' tuning and earphones, usable only by the skilful, patient, and enthusiastic) did not sell in large numbers. Nor did the first motor cars. Very often the big money remains to be made not by the pioneers but by the watchful improvers.

In no industry is this more true than publishing, and especially in periodicals. Since the spread of literacy in the second half of the nineteenth century, in the industrial countries, the market for reading matter has grown and has enriched those alert enough to exploit it, like Alfred Harmsworth, the Berry family, Lord Thomson of Fleet, and some hundreds of others far less well known.

In publishing, as in most manufacturing, it is the dynamic firm which keeps abreast of technology and lives, if not in the future, as far ahead in the present as wit and knowledge will allow, which takes the big prizes. The first 'daily magazine', the picture paper or tabloid, was not the radical innovation the first newspaper was. But it was an innovation in the sense that it opened a new market for newspapers, being a compromise between the solid letterpress of a daily paper devoted to news and the fully illustrated entertainment sheets or comics which appeared weekly and were directed at the semiliterate population, which was much more numerous than the truly literate.

Publishing, then, is an area in which one may expect most of the product innovations to be in the nature of imitations or improvements. But it must not be overlooked that this kind of product differs from all others in its dependence on two markets instead of one. Being a very high cost industry it does not sell its products at a price based on cost and profit calculations alone. With very few exceptions (one is probably *Private Eye*) a periodical or a newspaper derives a high proportion of its revenue from its advertisers as well as its buyers. In some newspapers the ratio is 60 per cent advertising revenue to 40 per cent sales revenue. If the cost of production is very high, as with a glossy magazine with a sewn binding and semi-stiff cover, it pays to restrict the circulation by charging a high price and appealing as closely as possible to the top 10 per cent of readers in terms of spending power.

Sometimes it pays to charge nothing at all for the journal, but to supply it free (and uninvited usually) to a carefully chosen list of potential readers whose interests are known to coincide with those of a group of advertisers. A number of trade and technical magazines now practise this policy, which has the advantages of avoiding a fluctuating circulation (the circulation is 'controlled', hence the term controlled circulation journal, CCJ) and of providing advertisers with a ready-made mailing list under the guise of a service to readers.

Of course, the advertiser's check on the efficacy of the journal is the response rate to his advertisements, but at the outset he has to take the publisher's word or that of his own media adviser for the selling potentialities of the new journal. In these cases, once the advertiser begins to be disillusioned about the usefulness to him of a particular journal, the end is near, unless the publisher and his editor can make the involuntary recipient actively interested in the contents.

All this may seem obvious to people acquainted with modern periodical publishing, but it remains an interesting aspect of product innovation, especially while publishers continue to launch new journals aimed at paid circulation. What follows is an account of such an attempt in the 1960s, when for various reasons the Thomson Organization, or rather one of its subsidiaries, decided that there ought to be a market for a new weekly magazine based on London, as the *New Yorker* was originally designed primarily for its parent city. This venture has been chosen because, on the face of it, the idea had much to commend it, the subsequent research confirmed that there was an adequate potential readership and that there would be satisfactory advertising support, but in the outcome the promise was not fulfilled, and it is instructive to consider why this should have been.

There were what might be called environmental restraints on the big British publishers in the 1960s, the Monopolies Commission having decreed that there should be no more takeovers of local newspapers. The Thomson Organization consequently turned its attention in other directions, one of them being the acquisition of a trade and technical group of journals, as this was then a growth area. A bid was therefore made for two profitable journals, the *Draper's Record* and *Men's Wear*, to form a nucleus. With this deal there came several other properties, including some printing works, which the Thomson management did not want and subsequently sold to the British Printing Corporation, the book publishers, Michael Joseph, and an old-established group of weekly glossy magazines, Illustrated London Newspapers Ltd. In the latter collection were the venerable *Illustrated London News*, the *Tatler*, and the *Sphere*, both rather snobbish 'society' weeklies with declining circulations.

The *Sphere* was quickly wound up, but both the *News* and the *Tatler* were kept going. The *Tatler* had been founded in 1901, when its appearance and contents were designed to please a rich segment of English society, with the emphasis on London 'society' and country-house living. Before the First World War the magazine lived mainly off its sales revenue, with advertising as jam on the bread and butter. Between the wars rising costs, both of production and distribution, and the loss of circulation brought about by price increases, pushed all such magazines towards increasing dependence on advertising revenue. By the time the *Tatler* came under the Thomson wing it was weak in both circulation and advertising.

An attempt to rebuild it to suit modern tastes produced little or no improvement. At that time the Thomson group had made another acquisition of relevance to this narrative. It was the Whitethorn Press, a group of county magazines, each with the generic label of *Life*, for example *Cheshire Life*, which prospered in that extremely prosperous county. There were Lancashire and Yorkshire magazines, too. Why not try out a *London Life?*

The idea had strong appeal for several reasons, one being that the country élite for whom the *Tatler* had been designed originally had given way, especially in the London and Home Counties region, to a suburban, 'stockbroker belt' class of big spenders, living in the country but working and often playing up in Town. No doubt they would buy a magazine which would keep them 'in touch', tell them what was going on in and around the capital, and provide them with social gossip and trendsetting chitchat.

One of the leading protagonists for converting the staid, older magazine into a more youthful, 'swinging' weekly was Mark Boxer, an ex-editor of *Granta*, the Cambridge student magazine, who had become the first editor of the *Sunday Times* colour magazine. He had developed a reputation for eye-catching artwork and bright ideas but, on his own admission, felt that by 1964 he had done all that he could for the colour magazine, limited as it was to sixty pages. He was ready to try his hand at something new and put forward his plans for the new magazine to the directors of Illustrated London Newspapers Ltd.

He conceived the new *London Life* as a leisure magazine with an active ingredient, which was in his words an approach to leisure 'through the mainstream of entertainment', using entertainment in the widest possible sense and not accepting the conventional definition as ranging across the arts and show business. It was to be aimed at both sexes with a bias towards women, presumably for commercial reasons as there is a lot of advertising to be picked up in fashion and beauty products, household appliances, and food. Like the *New Yorker*, *London Life* would have a city flavour but national, if not international, appeal. The influences would be the *New Yorker*, with 'showcase' (that is, prestige and not hard sell) advertising and the occasional 'long reads', *Vanity Fair*, American version, for its wit and the text-picture balance, *Elle* for visual originality, and the Sunday magazine of the *New York Herald Tribune* for youthful cosmopolitanism and an unglossy appearance. Mark Boxer visualized the new weekly as 'the antithesis of glossy', but in the end this idea was largely rejected on the grounds that prestige advertisements cannot be accommodated unless the medium is a glossy magazine which can take the artwork.

These were just preliminary ideas, and not all of them were accepted without modification. But there was one idea which appealed to most if not all of the ILN management. That was that the magazine should carry an events information section, giving times and dates, places and prices for everything going on in and around London from the cinema and theatre to racing and garden parties. The glossy magazine would therefore include a newsprint section, which could be printed late enough to be bang up to date and which incidentally would give an appearance of urgency to the whole thing, as well as toning down the too familiar glossiness.

The operation was to be broadly based, with fashion treated as news and not as feature material, with music taking in pop festivals as well as concerts and opera, with stock-car racing as well as standard motoring copy: in a phrase, the whole gamut of good living as it would appeal to the young, ambitious, energetic, and better-off or adventurous section of the urban and suburban population. Boxer, for one, wanted the weekly to break away from being just another journal competing for readers and advertisers and become a 'package' of amusements and services, indispensable to anyone lively enough to want to be in the swim, or with-it, to use the contemporary cant. In his memoranda about *London Life* he wrote, among other things, 'There should be something glamorous, even vulgar about *London Life* . . . It mustn't be self-consciously switched-on and patronise or dictate to its readers by telling them what they must think.' Nor, in spite of the long reads, was there to be too much writing. One long article an issue would be the most that readers would want, and such articles should have the quality of 'informative irony', such as could be found in the work of Truman Capote and Lillian Ross in the *New Yorker*, Terry Southern in *Esquire* and, ironically, the *Saturday Evening Post*'s 'Anatomy of a Flop', which Boxer planned to reprint.

The *New Yorker* was something of a guiding light. Later, when the new journal was faltering, Boxer recalled the words of Ross, the *New Yorker*'s first editor, quoted by James Thurber in his biography of the man: 'The *New Yorker* was the outstanding flop of 1925 . . . From an original run-off of 15,000 copies in February its circulation fell as low as 2,700 in August.' Nevertheless, it pulled round to become an international journal of high standing.

London Life began big with a print order of 100,000, against orders booked from wholesalers of 80,000. The first two issues sold about 50,000 each, but that total was never reached thereafter. By its sixth week sales were down to 25,000 and within a year it had stopped publication. The accumulated losses on the venture have never been made public but are estimated to have been of the order of £250,000. It was to avoid this drain of cash that the magazine was stopped after about forty issues. To have gone on with it would have been very costly and there seemed to be no sign of the upturn in sales that saved the *New Yorker*. Added to which there seems to have been some differences with the advertisers who felt that the *London Life* that was eventually published was not the prestige weekly in which they wanted to appear. In the words of a former Thomson senior executive, there was too much King's Road and Carnaby Street atmosphere and not enough Kensington and Knightsbridge.

There are always several reasons why a venture such as this fails and everyone who takes part has a different opinion. In the light of the research done under the Marketing Director of the group, the initial sales were highly satisfactory. Harry Henry, then the group marketing director, had made some calculations. Assuming that there were about two million families in Britain in 1964 who rated AB (the two highest income and ownership brackets conventionally used by market researchers), about half or one million would have a head of the household or a member between the ages of 19 and 45. This interesting condition was dictated by the concept of a young family, who were more likely to be in the forefront of fashion trends, and more inclined to favour something new.

About one-fifth of this million would be resident in Greater London and about one-third in the south-east region as a whole. Nearly two-thirds, in round figures 600,000, would live outside the south-east and the appeal of the magazine would be weakest for them. Rating the appeal of the magazine to Londoners at 6, to south-east residents at 3, and in the rest of the country at 1, Mr (now Professor) Henry extracted target circulations for the three areas of 12,000 in Greater London, 6,000 in the rest of the south-east, and 6,000 in the rest of Great Britain, a total of 24,000. Adding the so-called residual circulations which magazines of this type may expect to have (institutional, for example clubs, waiting-rooms and the like, overseas, and casual sales) brought the total target figure to 40,000. This was in the nature of being a minimal figure, and there was speculation as to the possibility of attaining a 6 per cent penetration nationally, which would produce a sales figure of 76,000, higher even than *Punch*, which was regarded as a close competitor.

While all such calculations are based on assumptions (that the magazine will sell at all, for instance) as well as facts, there was both experience and realism in the target figures. Thomson House had been through a similar exercise with *Family Circle*, a general interest magazine sold in supermarkets and shops from beside the cash register. Here the calculations had been based on numbers of outlets and numbers of customers checking out and the estimate and the actuality had been satisfactorily harmonious. *London Life* was a more difficult proposition because of a higher order of uncertainty. Nevertheless, the initial sales figures of 50,000 justified the calculations, even if it was only half the print order. It was the steep falling off in sales which was depressing. But there was also the dissatisfaction of advertisers.

The sequence of events leading up to the launch contains some significant details. The new magazine had been proposed in October 1964, but unanimous agreement to go ahead was not reached till the spring of the following year. The decision came at the end of April and from then on everything was done at high speed, particularly once the replacement of the familiar *Tatler* with a new journal had been leaked in the *Evening Standard* on 3 May.

In mid May there were inaugural lunches for advertisers and their agents at Elm House, the offices of Illustrated London Newspapers. Meanwhile the final key appointments were made to the staff. But the editorial offices did not begin to function till the end of June nearly six weeks after it became known that the planning of the magazine was under way. In early July there was a big party of space buyers, but no dummy was available until 10 August, because of printing difficulties. New journals often meet with initial printing snags, but with *London Life* they were made worse by the need to use two printers, one for the glossy sections and another for the newsprint information section. There was also a lot of colour work to be included. The dummy bore the launch date, 6 October, in big, bold type.

The quality of the dummy was such that some staff members asked for a postponement of the launch. This was refused on the grounds that it was a clear commitment. Then there arose internal dissension as to the 'copy platform', that is to say for whom the magazine was intended. There seems to have been two factions, and probably a lot of grey in between. One extreme saw the magazine in terms of 'swinging London', which was then all the rage. The other saw it in terms of what might be called Young Conservative, London-oriented suburbia, more likely to be seen at a point-to-point than a pop festival. Professor Henry looks back on it as a 'dichotomy' of viewpoints, which had developed almost without the antagonists being aware of it.

It is not difficult to see how this split could have arisen. On the one hand there were those who, having decided to replace the *Tatler*, were inclined to favour the formula of the successful Whitethorn series, which were akin to the old magazine in a number of ways. Then there were those, mainly on the editorial side, who thought that the new magazine must be as different as possible from the old. Otherwise, why do it? The management and the advertisement staff were naturally in favour of the young, prosperous suburbanite platform on which to approach one of the main revenue earners: an easier one to contact and persuade than the atomized, fickle, unknown potential readership. The editorial attitude tended to prevail, with the result that the first issue was not liked by the management and some of the advertisers. It could be inferred from the fact that sales held up in the early weeks that the buyers of the magazine did like it and that they fell off when the formula was directed more towards the older, safer pattern.

But there were other troubles. The price had been kept at 2*s.* 6*d.* (12½p), the only trace of the *Tatler* left except for a mention on the letter paper. With its information service for Londoners and suburbanites, comparison with the cheaper *What's On in London* was bound to be made. *What's On* then sold at 1*s.* (5p), a considerable price difference, but the cheaper magazine was smaller, simpler, and contained little editorial matter and little or no colour. It did, however, provide a more accurate information service than *London Life*, or so its editor, Kenneth Hurren, claimed in the issue after the launch of *London Life*, when he castigated his bigger rival for all its errors, giving chapter and verse. As a matter of fact, a number of Thomson people had tried to veto the information service at an early stage, being sceptical of its pulling power alongside the evening newspapers and *What's On*.

Interestingly enough, the average sales of the new weekly, after launching a day late on 7 October, settled down to a steady 25,000–26,000, a figure remarkably similar to the forecast made by Harry Henry if the residuals are left out. It is possible that these residual sales had not reached but might have reached the *Punch* level had the magazine's existence continued long enough for resistance to its unusual appearance been overcome (the title was subordinated to the date, to give an impression of urgency and novelty. This undoubtedly put some people off.).

The budgeted advertising had not on average been achieved, either. Instead of 80–84 pages an issue there had been about 60. Financial forecasts had predicted an 'investment' or loss on the journal of about £150,000 in the first full year, but when this figure looked like being doubled it seemed time to reconsider. After eight issues Mark Boxer was sent on leave and later transferred to other work. Around him had gathered most of the opprobrium generated by the failure of the enterprise, but his successors fared no better. In all probability when such a venture gets off to a bad start it is almost impossible for it to recover from the loss of interest and goodwill.

In October 1966, an ILN board meeting considered converting *London Life* to a monthly, for it was not a total failure, and was still maintaining a good sale even if its advertising revenue had shrunk somewhat. There were even signs that a turnround could be expected in 1967. But the ILN group was generally in low water with *Illustrated London News* itself not doing at all well. Another idea was to buy out *What's On* and merge the two, thus gaining both circulation and advertising goodwill (but how many *What's On* shillings would have been converted to half-crowns?). But the company owning *What's On* was taken over at this point, and another weekly information service, *Where To Go*, appeared, also at 1*s*., threatening to take over the *What's On* low-priced circulation if the merger took place.

During the discussions about continuing *London Life* as a monthly, some members of the ILN board voiced criticisms of the original formula. It had had too much of a 'boutique' image, it was thought, appealing not to the customers of the big department stores and the Bond Street emporia, and therefore to the businesses themselves as advertisers, but to the customers of the smaller, 'trendier' shops which did little if any advertising. The 'swinging London' set were not the readership originally envisaged by Harry Henry and was a departure from the original managerial brief. During the short life of the magazine attempts had been made, after a change of editor, to swing the contents and character more towards the AB London and suburban reader but by then too many advertisers were pulling out to make it worth while to continue the effort.

With such internal disagreement about a journal's audience it is impossible to hit both the circulation and advertising targets. And if you miss the first, you inevitably miss the second.

CASE

5 *Smoke gets in your eyes*

Not all product innovations are necessarily desired by the consuming public. Sometimes they are forced upon the public or sections of it 'for its own good', for example, car safety belts and motor-cyclists' crash helmets are now compulsory and will add to the cost of using a car or a motor-cycle. The fact that they benefit the users in the sense that they may save their lives or save them from serious injury plays a minor part in spreading their use voluntarily, even if a few wise individuals accept them without compulsion.

The Clean Air Act of 1956 similarly compelled people to use new products, mainly new fuels, in order to obey the rules of the clean air policy. People living in so-called smokeless zones were supposed to burn only 'authorized fuels'. If they had to change or improve their heating arrangements to burn such fuels they did receive some financial assistance from the local authority. If, however, they wanted to continue to use an open fire they would generally have needed to buy a kind of solid smokeless fuel known as 'reactive'. Such fuels, which bear names like Coalite and Rexco, while more efficient than coal are more expensive to buy, but at least they burn in open grates more or less like coal and thus appeal to the British tradition of the open fire. Official opinion was that the open fire could be preserved in spite of its inefficiency, and thus arose the need to help people conform to the Clean Air Act, by supplying them with cheap solid smokeless fuels.

From the Beaver Committee report on air pollution in 1954 to the present day, Parliament has never ceased questioning and debating the clean air policy and programme and the way in which it was continuously retarded by the lack of such a cheap, easily obtainable, easily burnt solid smokeless fuel in adequate quantities. There were, of course, many varieties of smokeless fuel available in the mid 1950s, from the by-product coke of the gas industry, which could not be burnt successfully in open grates, to the naturally smokeless or 'high rank' forms of coal including anthracite. Anthracite and other such coals have to be burnt in closed appliances, as for the most part does coke. Nevertheless, whenever the government was pressed about the shortage of smokeless fuels they usually fell back on the supply of coke from the gas industry. According to a 1963 report coke 'discouraged' the consumer because it is difficult to ignite, goes out if unattended, cannot be burnt in small grates with any success, and glows rather than flames, therefore not giving what some people would call a real fire. Also it is a bulky fuel to store and difficult to handle although light. These points were made in the *Report on Domestic Fuel Supplies and Clean Air Policy* (Cmnd 2231). This was the second report on the shortage of smokeless fuels, the first having been in 1960, the *Peech Committee Report on Solid Smokeless Fuels* (Cmnd 999).

At the time of the Peech Committee the North Western Gas Board was trying to make smokeless briquettes from 'fines' (small coal) and the National Coal Board was experimenting with briquetting coal dust after heating it in a fluidised bed (that is, suspending the coal dust in a hot draught) and without using a binder. The idea of 'binderless briquetting' was to avoid the use of tar which adds to the smokiness of the coal. It also enables the use of low rank coal 'fines'. In other words, low price and virtually unusable coal dust could be converted into a smokeless premium fuel, an appealing idea to the Coal Board who were faced with the dwindling use of pulverized fuel in electrical power stations which were being converted to oil, and under increasing pressure from the government of the day to fill the annual gap in the winter supply of smokeless fuels to smoke control areas.

The unfortunate consumer living in a 'smokeless' area was theoretically obliged to avoid the use of any but 'authorized' fuels. He was naturally mainly interested in adequate space heating in the home in winter, although there must have been a proportion of consumers who realized the benefits of clean air once they began to enjoy them. Before the coming of the Clean Air Act the Beaver Committee had estimated that an average family would spend between £30 and £40 a year on cleaning materials, laundry bills, and so on as a consequence of air pollution by smoke, mainly from domestic chimneys. According to a debate recorded in *Hansard* (4 February 1955, column 1446) it would take ten years to achieve an 80 per cent reduction in the pollution of the atmosphere. The Clean Air lobby led at that time by Mr (now Sir) Gerald Nabarro, had tabled a Bill in 1955 only to withdraw it in favour of the government measure. The problem which was created for the National Coal Board was to replace the 19 million tons of house coal burnt every year in 'black areas' by some form of smokeless fuel. With the supply of all types of solid smokeless fuels calculated in 1956 at just over 7 million tons the estimated gap in supply if house coal were banned wholly or for the most part would be between 10 and 12 million tons. This was presumably why the 1956 Act did not make the adoption of smoke control orders by local authorities obligatory. This left the consumer in the position of being compelled in some areas to buy and burn a fuel for which, if he could get it, he had to pay more than house coal, while others, especially miners, continued to burn smoky coal.[1] There were many complaints in the House of Commons by members that their constituents disliked this situation, and the Peech Committee was convened after the smokeless fuel shortage in the cold winter of 1958, when the actual consumption of solid smokeless fuels had been just over 5½ million tons.[2] The Peech Committee was highly optimistic and forecast a supply in 1961 of over 10,700,000 tons of solid smokeless fuels, a prediction which seemed to take no account of such things as the diminishing supply of coke as gas works converted to oil and the slowness of the Coal Board to succeed with its promising char briquetting process. The Peech Committee forecast for 1965 of over 12 million tons looks ludicrous beside the actual figure in 1969–70 of just over 8,100,000.

Three years later the situation was reviewed again and one or two facts bobbed to the surface. First, the gas industry had helped to create the shortage by changing over from coal to oil using the new ICI process of steam reforming. Secondly, it appeared that official opinion had held that oil was unlikely to be widely used domestically but the oil industry had taken steps to see that it was, in the form of oil central heating. A point made in the 1963 report was that the successful development of the clean air programme depended upon an adequate supply of smokeless fuels. The Peech Committee calculations, which predicted a surplus of smokeless fuel by 1965, had in fact concealed the more complex truth that this would be a surplus

1. Miners' coal in 1956 was 5·3 million tons, about one-seventh of national domestic consumption.

2. The missing 2 million was probably available as coke but unusable on open fires.

for closed appliances only but for open fires both improved and unimproved there would be a shortage of 2 million tons. The Committee expressed the hope that the Coal Board's 'tentative plans' would take care of this.

By this time the makers of premium smokeless fuels had seen their sales rise by 1,300,000 tons a year, while bituminous coal consumption had fallen by 3 million tons. Great hope was officially expressed that the Coal Board's 'Birch Coppice Process' would provide 600,000 tons a year of open fire briquettes (see below). These were the famous 'Bronowski briquettes' made by the binderless char briquetting process and the 600,000 tons was to come not from their £9 million pilot-plant at Birch Coppice but from a new full-scale commercial plant at Coventry.

Looking back over the *Hansard* debates and the many question and answer sessions one cannot help noting that government spokesmen, whether Labour or Conservative, always insisted that smokeless fuel supplies were adequate: usually in the summer. In the autumn it was customary to reply that 'the situation might be tight in some areas and for some fuels'. There can be no doubt that the smoke control programme was consistently hampered by the failure of the coal industry to provide sufficient quantities of smokeless fuel, in spite of the move towards central heating which was encouraged by the suppliers of fuel and power and resulted in 40 per cent of British dwellings having some form of central heating by 1970, a trend which was gradually reducing the market for open fire smokeless fuels.

A report on the Protection of the Environment in May 1970 (Cmnd 4373) noted that the shortage of smokeless fuel still persisted after fifteen years, that the coke shortage had meant the maintenance in being of unprofitable gas works, but that the Labour Government nevertheless intended to apply the Clean Air Act of 1968 (a Private Member's Bill originating from Mr Robert Maxwell) which gave it power to compel 'laggard local authorities in badly polluted areas to make smoke control orders . . . when this temporary difficulty has been overcome'. In the winter of 1970 it became necessary to suspend smoke control orders and on 15 March 1971 it was stated in the House that 810 orders had been partly or wholly suspended, of which 331 were in Greater London.

In the report of the Domestic Coal Consumer Council, 31 October 1970, a shortage of solid smokeless fuel was predicted for the coming winter, and blame for this was placed by Mr Peter Walker, Minister for the Environment, on the Labour Government (*Hansard*, 25 November 1970, column 386). The previous February, Mr Christopher Chataway had tabled a motion to 'deplore the failure of Her Majesty's government to ensure the supplies of smokeless fuel necessary to implement the clean air policy', but Mr Harold Lever, the Labour Government spokesman, had refused to recognize that there was a shortage, except in some localities and of some types.

These are the bare bones, the skeleton of the story in which the unfortunate Coal Board was cast in the role of scapegoat. There is little point in laying the blame on any particular institution or individual. If one wanted to be extreme, one could say that both the discomfiture of the consumer in a cold winter in a smokeless zone and the Coal Board's estimated investment of £40 million in a process which failed to fulfil its promise on time, were the result of fifty years campaigning by the National Smoke Abatement Society, now called the National Clean Air Society. Or one could place the blame upon the clean air lobby, stimulated by the London smog of 1952 which is alleged to have killed 4,000 old and infirm people. Whatever explanation one prefers to adopt, the truth of the matter would seem to be that there was a total lack of co-ordination between the political lobbies, the Civil Service, and the fuel and power industries, just as there appears to have been no phasing of the clean air programme either chronologically or geographically to fit in with the availability of fuels. It has even been argued that the Government emasculated the 1956 Act, and was less than half-hearted about its clean air policy. The bickerings about smokeless fuels were therefore mainly political sniping.

The fact remains that several hundred thousand families were inconvenienced and even seriously discomfited in a series of cold winters, with resultant nagging in Parliament and in the Press, leading to constant pressure on the NCB to come up as quickly as possible with Dr Jacob Bronowski's 'magic bullets'. Thus was an innovation forced into being at great cost and with much tribulation at the NCB. The following narrative sketches their part in the story.

The Clean Air Act requirements demand a fuel with a high calorific value and yet one that will burn without a high emission of dark smoke. Fuels such as Coalite and Rexco are produced by carbonizing or 'coking' high-quality coal, and between them these two brands supply about 2 million tons a year of smokeless fuel for burning in open fires or 'openable room heaters'. They are, of course, more expensive than untreated domestic coal and people would not have used them in large quantities but for local orders made under the Clean Air Act.

Before the Act itself several local authorities had secured local Acts and gone 'smokeless' and the NCB had assisted them to some extent by using a 1940 process to produce Phurnacite using high-rank coal, with tar as a binder. With the coming of the Act in 1956 demand for smokeless fuels for open fires was bound to soar, so that lower-grade coal would have to be used. A lot of coal cut mechanically tends to be small and to have a high volatile content, which simply means that it is smokier than 'high-rank' coal which contains less than 20 per cent volatile matter[1] (anthracite and Welsh steam coal are almost free from smoky elements and can be heated with little or no loss of weight). The problem was to convert this small coal into a solid lump or briquette by compression and then to remove some of the volatile matter by heating, thus creating an acceptable open fire fuel.

The main part in the production of such a low-cost reactive domestic fuel at the NCB was played by Dr Bronowski, in the early years at least. He had joined the Board under Dr Idris Jones, Director-General of Research in the 1950s, and the Board Member for Science, Sir Charles Ellis, whose policy was to recruit scientists.

Idris Jones had already introduced Phurnacite as a smokeless premium fuel, made from high-rank coal by a French process. Bronowski, who was in charge of coal chemistry at the Coal Research Establishment (newly hived off from the old Central Research Establishment which had included mining research) became interested in the production of a high efficiency fuel for the steel industry.

He had been examining the inefficiency of coking. Fourteen hours to convert one charge of coal produced hard coke outside and soft at the core because of the uneven heat soak, coal being a good insulator. Coking is better done on small pieces, ideally on powder. The NCB had sent a chemist to the Massachusetts Institute of Technology, and he had brought back the notion of using a fluidized bed technique, in which finely and evenly ground coal is burnt suspended in a hot air draught. The hot gases leave the reactor at the top and the tar collects in the bottom. Volatile matter can be removed to any desired percentage by controlling the residence time.

The next step is to compress the char, as the carbonized coal dust is called, into uniformly sized pieces. The idea of using the hot char's

1. Twenty per cent was the Beaver Committee minimum for volatile content.

plasticity to make a binderless briquette has been described as 'beautiful but fatal'. It was not Bronowski's idea. Direct briquetting from the fluidized bed came to be a will-o'-the-wisp pursued manfully by the NCB for many years.

To hold the fragments together in a shaped piece it had been thought necessary to use a binding material, but that method increases the smokiness of the fuel before it goes through the heating process. The Coal Research Establishment had therefore applied itself at first to the problem of binderless briquetting, using very high pressure to force the coal granules together.

This line of thought led to the method known as Shape. Dr H. R. Gregory, then Senior Scientist at the Coal Research Establishment, Stoke Orchard, said in a paper to the Institute of Fuel on 23 March 1960, that binderless briquetting had been tried previously, using fine grinding of the coal and extremely high pressures up to 15 tons per square inch, making the process very costly. The Shape process, developed at a Cardiff plant, assisted the cohesion of the coal granules by adding 'shear' to the direct pressure, which in practice meant giving a sideways stress to the material at the peak of direct pressure.

The complete treatment of the coal included handling, drying, pressing, and briquette handling. The capital cost of the Cardiff plant was estimated as £577,000 a year to handle 125,000 tons, a cost per ton of £4. 12*s*. without adding in the cost of the original coal, which at that time may have been about 30*s*. per ton. But what seems to have brought the work on Shape to a standstill was the discovery that after briquetting the dust formed by the fuel when handled and stored was so fine that it behaved almost like an aerosol and took a long time to settle, a characteristic which could have proved to be a great nuisance in the home.

At the time that Dr Gregory was writing, work was therefore going ahead on the application of the Shape technique to char briquetting, in other words not going back to the use of a binder but using higher pressures to make a completely smokeless product out of treated coal dust. 'The carbonisation of low-rank coal in a fluid bed', wrote Dr Gregory, 'followed by binderless briquetting of the char to form a premium smokeless domestic fuel is an application of great promise; more will be heard of it . . .' And indeed a lot more was to be heard of it, as this was the basic process developed at Stoke Orchard by Dr Bronowski, whose name became synonymous with the briquettes or 'bullets' as the Press nicknamed them.

At that time Dr Bronowski's deputy was Dr D. C. Rhys-Jones, who contributed an article to the *New Scientist* in 1959 (7 May) outlining the work of the Coal Research Establishment on smokeless fuels, from Phurnacite, with its binder and high temperature carbonization, to the fluid-bed carbonized, binderless fuels briquetted either on the Shape extrusion press or on more conventional roll presses. In 1959–60 experiments at Birch Coppice (a colliery between Tamworth and Atherston) led to the replacement of roll-presses by extrusion presses of a kind which had been tried out at Cardiff during the Shape experiments. This pilot plant seems to have been something of a failure. The fuel used was low-rank coal, carbonized and briquetted without a binder on an extrusion press. The difficulties encountered were numerous. Apart from high cost, the briquettes, which were the early version of the brand known as Homefire, designed for open fires, were difficult to store, because they developed a high moisture content like some types of coke, they had a tendency to spontaneous combustion in storage, and there was heavy wear on the press. They were also liable to break during handling and transport. It was also found that the coal granules became minute plastic 'balloons' as the gases inside them expanded. These inflated granules resisted pressure and had to be flattened by using shear.

This process is now used in a modified version to manufacture Homefire at the Coal Board plant at Coventry. The target for 1971–2 was 200,000 tons, but the 1969–70 output was a mere 60,000 tons. Nevertheless, the Coal Board remains convinced that the Coventry plant will succeed eventually, although Mr Wilfred Miron, chairman of the Midlands and South Wales Board said in April 1970, that Coventry and Markham (Doncaster) were 'disappointing failures' (*Financial Times*, 29 April 1970). The 1972–3 output was 200,400 tons.

Looking back it is rather surprising to the outsider that the NCB should have decided to lay down still another experimental plant, this time to make Roomheat, a char briquette similar to Homefire but for use in openable room heaters rather than open fires, also at Birch Coppice. Both pilot plants were begun in August 1957, and both had, to put it mildly, chequered careers. In spite of all the difficulties, however, the Board, urged on by governmental pressure eventually went ahead with two full-scale plants.

Markham I, as the first plant was called, cost about £750,000 to build. Sophisticated control techniques were applied to this project, particularly network planning on the PERT principle (Programme Evaluation and Review Technique). In spite of all this the plant suffered a serious breakdown during early running and was eventually abandoned in favour of a second plant, Markham II, which had been started at a cost of over £1 million before Markham I was complete. Even more surprising than this decision to put in hand a second Roomheat plant before proving the first one, was the fact that even at this advanced stage the integrated pilot plant at Stoke Orchard had not been put into full operation.

Working on the Stoke Orchard plant it had been discovered that the cooling stage of the process, after the briquettes had been through the roll press, prevented them from catching fire when stacked for storage, which they did if they were simply piled up hot, as the Birch Coppice team had already found out apparently, but not in time to warn the Markham team, who were taken by surprise at the spontaneous combustion of their product. Another snag which had been discovered in the mechanical handling of Homefire briquettes was that there was a loss by disintegration of as much as 10–11 per cent by weight. This was a serious loss both in production and in the waste of value-added during the fairly costly briquetting process.

It can be seen already that up to the mid 1960s the Coal Board had invested a great deal of money in research and development on five sites: pilot plants at Stoke Orchard, the Shape plant at Cardiff, the two Markhams at Doncaster, a pilot plant at Birch Coppice, and the Coventry plant.

The initial cost of Markham I was added to by two rebuildings which were necessitated by poor original design data. This data had apparently been provided by Stoke Orchard on the basis of pilot scale work but it was not 'hard' design information as far as the scaled-up process was concerned. There was a similar information lag between Birch Coppice and Coventry, in that the Birch Coppice plant had had a severe problem of wear in the 140 presses being used for briquetting. The abrasiveness of coal dust at a pressure of 6 tons per square inch meant that there was almost always some of the plant undergoing replacement or repair. As late as 1967 the Coventry plant was still undergoing modification because of the problem of distributing the output of the carbonizers to a much larger number of presses.

In the Beaver Committee Report on Clear Air it was insisted that a fuel should be regarded as smokeless only if it contained less than 20 per cent volatile matter. The Midlands Phurnacite was higher than that in volatile content, hence the search for a really low smoke fuel, which led the Coal Board through such long and tortuous projects. Carbonizing had previously been practised mainly on already briquetted fuels. Dr Rhys Jones's idea had been to briquette after carbonizing and there is no doubt that the principle is sound, it is the large-scale practice that turns out to present difficulties. These difficulties were complicated by the official obligation to produce as speedily as possible, if not a smokeless fuel, then one lower in volatile content than seemed to be attainable when starting from low-rank coal.

In 1970 when the then chairman of the Coal Board, Lord Robens, announced that there would still be a shortage of 700,000 tons of solid smokeless fuel, that the Board would be importing about 80,000 tons of French briquettes made from anthracite 'duff' (a coarse dust exported to France in large quantities) and that he was recommending the suspension of new smoke control orders, there was an outcry, led by the Consumer Council. At the same time the Gas Council was ordered to maintain in being five gas works which it had been going to close down for reasons of economy, so as to prevent further reductions in the supply of coke for domestic consumption. Lord Robens himself had used the term 'broken biscuits' of what Bronowski regarded as a twentieth-century fuel for twentieth-century homes. Bronowski regarded most of the criticisms of the briquettes as marginal and trivial, the carpings of minds conditioned to resist change.

After fourteen years of effort to produce a smokeless briquetted fuel for burning in traditional open fires and openable room heaters, demand, created almost entirely by the clean air legislation, had continued to outstrip supply by a large quantity. It is a sharp lesson in innovation planning, the obvious moral of which is that you cannot order innovations into being to a timetable. There are, of course, much wider implications, notably in the area of fuel policy, where co-ordination between the various forms of fuel and energy supply could at least have averted some of the unbalanced situations which led to unnecessary and wasteful competition between the public corporations involved, including the notorious battles between the the Gas and Electricity Councils over the connection charges made by the latter. This was a scheme for waiving the connection charge for new dwellings if a local authority or developer agreed to forego gas mains connections.

The significance of the connection charge tactic is that it came at a time when the various suppliers were fighting to win a share of the central heating market, a growth sector in the 1960s invaded by coal, gas, oil, electricity, the appliance makers, and the finance houses, not to mention a variety of contractors. The increase in the number of households having some kind of central heating installation was bound to eat into the market for solid smokeless fuels intended for burning in open grates.[1] Without this development the gap between the demand for such fuels and the supply would have been even wider. It was partly the absence of an adequate supply that compelled the government of the day to make the first Clean Air Act enabling rather than compulsory, so that as local authorities opted to apply the Act, the supply of fuels and the adaptation of grates, for example the provision of gas pokers for ignition of fuels less combustible than coal, could be stepped up. The 1968 Act's Section 8, Smoke Control Areas, can only be regarded as unrealistic in the light of NCB experience.[2]

Ironically, while Britain underwent its almost perennial regional winter shortages of suitable smokeless fuels during the 1960s, the French were running a surplus, having apparently hit on a process of oxidization of coal which not only reduced the volatile content but, instead of baking it off, as with the original Phurnacites, converted it into solid combustible fractions. The Coal Board were, however, deeply committed to char briquetting using fluid bed techniques and there seemed to be no theoretical reason why it should not work, as indeed they are now demonstrating in practice.

1. Current estimates show that 60 per cent of dwellings now have some form of centra heating.

2. Under Section 9(i) it became illegal to buy, sell, or deliver 'unauthorised fuels' in a declared smokeless area.

CASE

6 *The breakthrough that went broke*

This chapter was completed months before Du Pont's announcement (18 March 1971) that they had decided to withdraw Corfam. The losses now amount to about $250 million.

The calculation which encouraged E. I. Du Pont de Nemours to back their 'poromeric' shoe-leather substitute Corfam was what might be called global. Demographic trends showed that the world population increase was moving at a rate likely to create a demand for shoes that could not be met from the products of the hide-bearing animal population. True, much of this increase was in the developing countries where climate, poverty, and habit conspire to make the wearing of shoes either superfluous, incongruous, or out of reach. With growing affluence in these countries, however, the forecasters considered that taste and means would one day turn in the direction of acquiring if not actually wearing such 'civilized' things as shoes.

According to the various published histories of Corfam, the origins of the idea of such a material, having all the admirable qualities of leather without some of the defects, such as cracking, scarring, and drying out if not 'fed' with polishes containing waxy substances, can be traced to before the Second World War, the 1930s in fact, according to Mr William D. Lawson writing in *Research Management* in 1965.[1] The company is also said to have been 'aware of the need and potential market for a material, with properties equal to or preferably better than leather' for 'perhaps as long as fifty years'.[2]

For our purpose the year 1955 will serve, as it was in that year that the New Venture was initiated that was to lead to Corfam and its arrival on the United States market in 1964. Du Pont had a long

1. Lawson, W. D., Lynch, C. A., and Richards, J. C., 'Corfam: Research brings chemistry to footwear', *Research Management*, 8, no. 1 (1965).

2. Jenkins, G. I., and Drinkwater, H. G., 'Corfam versus cowhide', *The Director* (May 1969).

experience of synthetic film and sheet manufacture, even before the 1930s. During those years they developed a synthetic shoe upper material trade-marked Pateena, so the footwear industry was no stranger to them when they attempted in the 1950s to develop and sell to that industry a material that would break down its resistance and the public's to 'plastics'.

The official account by Lawrence Lessing of *Fortune*[1] describes the 1930s development work at Du Pont's Central Research Department on the deposition of synthetic polymers in layers to make a permeable composite sheet. The work was delayed by wartime commitments, but by 1953 three departments of the company were once again experimenting. Textile Fibers was working on the suitability of particular man-made fibres for the making of the needle-web, or bat, which is the basis of the material (patents were taken out for parts of this process as early as 1948–9). Films Department and Fabrics and Finishes Department were looking at sheet structure simultaneously. This was deliberately competitive research and development.

It was in 1955 that the Executive Committee, reviewing technical budgets and reports, decided that from the next year Fabrics and Finishes should have the sole responsibility for the development of the new material. At that time, there already existed two small-scale plants for making pieces of the new material, but up to that point no-one was satisfied as to the physical or aesthetic qualities of the samples from the Fabrics and Finishes pilot plant, but the Film Department's product was, while still far from perfect, somewhat preferred.

Field tests were begun, using both lots of samples at first, in 1956 and continued into 1957, by which time it began to appear that the Fabrics and Finishes technology had the better chance of being refined eventually into a saleable product. So far, so good, but, as Dr John C. Richards remarks, 'As is usually the case early in development, our laboratory tests had not been calibrated against performance of the material in actual use.'[2] This problem of performance in use, especially of a material intended to survive the kind of treatment that consumers inflict on footwear, proved to be something of a trap for one or two of Corfam's rivals, some time after the Du Pont development team had met and overcome a whole series of obstacles

1. Lessing, Lawrence, *The Fast Footrace of Corfam* (Du Pont, 1966).
2. 'Stepping lively to keep Corfam ahead', *Chemical Week* (23 September 1967).

to acceptance. And acceptance had to be gained at three levels: the manufacturers had to be shown how to work with the synthetic; retailers had to be warned about at least one important characteristic, that Corfam does not stretch; and shoppers needed reassurance that this was not just another 'plastic'.

Du Pont had, therefore, put in four years of 'mission-oriented' research and development before setting out to discover whether the new material would be both practicable and acceptable, which is a testimonial either to their willingness and capability to take big risks or to their confidence in the R & D, probably both.

Jenkins and Drinkwater admit that all this work had provided 'only meagre clues' as to the precise formula that would be needed when they went into large-scale manufacture. At this stage the 'venture group' had examined the American footwear market and found that to be competitive, that is to capture and retain a significant proportion of the 1,000 million square feet of leather needed for the 600 million pairs of shoes that constituted the US market, they would need a range of at least four finishes. A suede finish was what they aimed at first, because it requires a shorter process than the smooth, grained, or shiny finishes which constitute the rest of the market. The smooth, or 'calf' finish, is the most popular. The suede or napped effect does not require the basic material to be coated with a polymer before being dyed and embossed. The surface is treated to give the suede effect and then dyed.

Unfortunately, this line of development was nipped off in 1956–7 by a combination of high cost (a polyester fibre of less than 2 denier was needed to get near enough to animal fibre, which is of the order of 0·1 denier or less) and unexpected competition from Hush Puppies, brushed pigskin shoes made from surplus pig hides from the Chicago meat-packing stations. Market research also revealed the odd fact that the popularity of suede shoes with the American public has a cycle swinging over six or seven years. It was not that they were on the wrong point of the cyclic curve. Looking ahead, Du Pont realized that their new material was going to be fairly costly unless it was made in continuous big volume. A cyclical product was not what they wanted.

The 'grain' leather market, the smooth and embossed finishes, was more stable and much larger. To arrive at a suitable product was bound to be costlier, because of the additional coating and finishing stages. In 1960, however, it was decided to build a pilot plant incorporating those stages. At this point in the history of Corfam it was important for the company to be able to manufacture sufficient quantities of the material to make 'field tests'. This meant in practice that enough Corfam had to be made to supply shoemakers with sufficient quantities to make a large sample of trial pairs. As a by-product of this experience at 'semi-works' scale, enough design information should be forthcoming to equip the Engineering Department to perform the upscaling of the plant from sound basic data.

In the United States the footwear market, according to figures used and published by Du Pont, is divided into 47 per cent women's shoes, 20 per cent children's, 18 per cent men's, and 15 per cent athletic and other. More than two-thirds of the market consists of shoes made of smooth or grained leather. From these percentages it seemed most economical for Du Pont to aim at the women's market, and at the fashionable segment rather than at selling run-of-the-mill street shoes. Their first aim was to introduce Corfam into high-priced footwear for both women and men, but they concentrated on the women's end of the market. A careful study of women's shoe-buying habits revealed that generally there are two classes of purchase. On the one hand a woman buys comfortable shoes for habitual wear, for shopping and for wearing all day. The permeability of such shoes is important, for although as she walks around her feet 'pump' air and moisture out of the shoe, when she sits down the moisture accumulates.

In addition to the need for good permeability, such shoes need 'stress decay': they have to be able to conform to the shape of the foot, as fitting and size are always approximate. It was known from the start that Corfam did not have the properties required: it was not as permeable as natural leather, and it did not stretch at all. It was therefore more suitable for the other type of purchase, the shoes bought to match an outfit, not used for heavy wear, and discarded before they are worn out.

Du Pont also realized how difficult it was to control all the stages through which the shoes would have to go before reaching the wearer. Even with an almost perfect upper material, the comfort and quality of the shoes would depend upon what lining and other components were chosen by the manufacturer. A non-permeable lining would cancel out the porous properties of Corfam. To check on this a team of technical advisers was created to work with the manufacturers, to advise them about such matters as heat setting for shape preservation, not necessary with leather, but also to make sure that Corfam was not combined with unsuitable ancillary materials.

It is now part of the general history of Corfam that more than 200 different shoe manufacturing plants in the United States, using a wide range of shoemaking machinery, made nearly 20,000 trial pairs of shoes, which were then tested together with control samples of leather shoes, so that each subject wore a Corfam shoe on one foot and a leather one on the other, without being told which was which. All kinds of occupational groups were included in the trials, postmen and policemen being the hardest on footwear.

Alongside these extensive tests Du Pont employed a team of psychologists from a university to look into foot comfort. The 'Comfort Report' submitted to the company indicated that the footwear market divides evenly into three categories of individual: those whose feet always hurt (dubbed 'augmentors'); those whose feet never hurt ('reducers'); and those who come somewhere in between. What was worrying the marketing men was the possibility that discomfort might, because of careless fitting in the shoe shop, come to be associated with their product. Most styles of women's shoes have to fit closely to stay on, and shop assistants sometimes persuade a woman to take a smaller size and 'break it in' for this reason. With Corfam such advice would be misleading and eventually harmful to the product as well as the customer's feet, perhaps.

So attention had to be paid to the education of the retailers as well as the manufacturers, with the added difficulty that the commission-rewarded assistant is unlikely to 'sell' Corfam when it needs to be carefully explained when leather is available and familiar. The burden of all this detailed marketing was borne by the Poromeric Products Division of the Fabrics and Finishes Department, set up in November 1962, and headed by a 'venture manager' who had responsibility for the whole sequence of activities from research through engineering and production to sales.

It was important for him and his colleagues to learn thoroughly the industry which they were 'invading', leather tanning and shoemaking. While it was relatively easy to get on working terms with a group of leading manufacturers, and also to learn the identities of the leading retailers in the major selling areas of the United States, the feedback from customers, whose repeat orders and word-of-mouth recommendations would determine the long-run fate of Corfam, was a longer process. Field tests and market surveys could help to shorten the 'feedback loop', but it was difficult to get a clear picture of customer reaction from the retail trade as, when questioned, they tended merely to repeat complaints.

There could be no question that the Du Pont team explored every possibility that might affect public acceptance of their product, and from 1964 their efforts seemed to have been handsomely rewarded. Beginning with a year's sale of one million pairs, by 1968 over 40 million were selling in the United States alone. Growth had been almost geometric, doubling each year, until 1969 when it looked as if a plateau had been reached. Also the Du Pont campaign in Europe had not been as successful as had been expected, with the result that a new finishing plant in Malines, Belgium, was closed down.

Early in 1970 a story in the American journal *Oil, Paint and Drug Reporter*, repeated in the February issue of the British *Rubber Journal*, and said to be based on an interview with Du Pont executives, claimed that Corfam had still to recoup $80 million of the original investment, and that its high cost meant that any extension of its markets would lead to still greater losses. The story also said that the company now realized that it had been mistaken in aiming at the expensive end of the market in the first place, and had now lost the chance of exploiting the lower ranges of prices.

One reason that has been given for this setback is 'sailing ship effect'. The term was coined by S. C. Gilfillan in his book *Inventing the Ship* (1935), in which he pointed out that all the greatest improvements in the design of sailing ships had come after the invention and development of the steamship. Similarly, once the leather tanners had grasped the threat of Corfam and its followers they set about giving leather some of the advantages claimed for the synthetics, and also did their best to get the cost of leather down. That this did have some effect on Corfam's market penetration does not seem in doubt.

There was, however, another factor, much less easily foreseen, which Du Pont executives now recognize was decisive in shutting them off from a large segment of the women's shoe market. It was the sudden popularity of polyvinylchloride, PVC. PVC is an impermeable plastic material, which is why it has been used for waterproof clothing. It was the last form of synthetic sheet that Du Pont chemists might expect to become a rival to their precious poromeric in the footwear market. But it did.

There were several 'reasons' for this event. First, came the series of footwear fashion changes associated with the miniskirt. Boots were one form of acceptable accompaniment to the very short skirt worn over tights, the other was a flat or medium-heeled shoe with a 'chunky' profile. There was a multitude of styles, but one thing they had in common: shoes for young women are more open, more 'ventilated' than shoes for older women or for men. With open heels, toes, and sides, or sandal patterns, there is less need for porosity in the upper material.

At the same time, a shiny black shoe became popular, which at first seemed a boon to the makers of Corfam, who had been planning a 'shining' version of Corfam, and they did succeed in capturing the top segment of this market. But most of the rest went to the vinyls, first in imitation black patent, then in colours, and later with the so-called 'wet look'.

The hold of the vinyls was strengthened by their extreme cheapness and the fact that, with constant and varied style changes demanded by the 'trend-setters' and their imitators, they could be bought one month and thrown away the next after intensive use without any great financial loss. Corfam was too durable as well as too expensive. Indeed, at one stage in the early history of Corfam its strength was included among its advantageous qualities. While durability is a quality that has always appealed to the thrifty, the conservative, and those whose response to fashion fluctuates by decades rather than seasons, it is irrelevant when all that the customer wants is something up-to-the-minute, inexpensive, and ephemeral. In the age of disposables and planned obsolescence durability is no longer a plus.

There have been and are a number of types of Corfam, some more complex in their construction than others, but none made from only one layer of lamination. A rival to Corfam which appeared in 1968 was Porvair, a porous plastic sheet that had originally been developed as a separator material for use in lead-acid accumulators (car starter batteries). A one-layer synthetic, it had not occurred to its inventors, Chloride Electrical Storage Company, that it might have another use until Corfam was launched. Porvair was one of many competing products that also nibbled away at the markets for which Corfam was intended, but even collectively they did far less damage than the arrival of that familiar but overlooked plastic, PVC.

Even now Corfam cannot be written off as a total failure, because it did not recover its investment in a mere six years on the market.

A large-scale, high technology product can take decades to pay off, and eventually Corfam could break even and begin to earn profits for its owners. The big question for the student of this situation is, what went wrong? Du Pont had analysed the market in every conceivable way. They had looked at the breakdown of the market by sex and by age: but only as regards 'adults' and 'children' where there seemed to be a distinct teenage sector. They had divided the women's market into fashion and non-fashion. They had looked at the psychology of comfort.

Perhaps the gap in the data was the absence of any analysis of the women's fashion market by age and income group: which might have revealed the teenage and twenties growing preference for cheap, throwaway shoes, regardless of comfort, permeability, and all those factors Du Pont had gone to such trouble to examine. Here is a case, and by no means an isolated one, where the product may have proved to be 'too good' for an important fraction of its intended market.

As a final comment which may have a bearing on the difficulties encountered by Du Pont in the marketing of Corfam, Fig. 6.1 is worth study. Based on figures from the American Footwear Manufacturers' Association (reprinted with permission from *The Economist* of 27 June 1970) it shows that the domestic market for footwear was contracting all through the crucial years of Corfam's development and launch. Although the total supply of footwear to the American market exceeded 800 million pairs in 1969 as compared with 600 million on average from 1960 onwards, the difference was made up by imports.

In 1960 4 per cent of shoes sold in the United States were made abroad. Now it is over 25 per cent. And these imports are of women's dress ('fashion') shoes and the more expensive men's shoes, two segments of the market at which Corfam was aimed. The result has been that a lot of footwear factories in Massachusetts, a centre of the industry, have had to close. As many as fifteen plants a year were closing down when *The Economist* reported. About 50,000 jobs in the industry had been lost nationally. This was in Corfam's home market.

Two main reasons have been given. Foreign shoes are cheaper because of lower labour costs. Also American manufacturers make too many lengths and widths and consequently have high production costs and high wastage because of excessive variety. How much of the 200 million pairs of imports are made from Corfam or its rivals

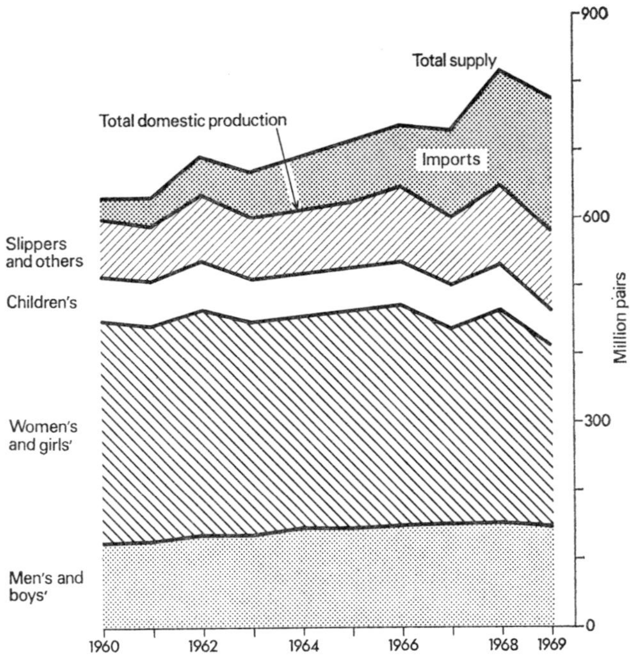

Fig. 6.1. Shoes for Americans. *Source* American Footwear Manufacturers' Association.

and in particular, Clarino, is not known, although it appears that a high proportion of these imports came from Japan.

In the light of these hindsight revelations Corfam's sales performance in the United States domestic market is all the more remarkable. The steep growth in sales between 1964 and 1969 can now be seen against a background of increasing import pressures. But in fact most if not all of these imports were not aimed at the market sectors initially selected for Corfam by the Du Pont management. The importers were invading the sectors scheduled for Corfam's low-cost, long-run future development and diffusion.

If this realization teaches anything it must be that marketing research must be broader-based than it is, with information about potential substitutes ranging across industrial divisions and international frontiers, particularly in the case of really radical and high-cost innovations. There can be little doubt that the Du Pont leadership and its advisors did all that they thought necessary to establish both the existence of a growing market for their technology and also the acceptance of their product at all levels of that potential market. With that special wisdom conferred by hindsight we can now suggest that perhaps even this effort was not enough.

CASE

7 *Its bloom is shed*

'John Bloom, a young and brilliant businessman, entirely self-made and not so much self-taught as untaught . . .' is how Bernard Levin describes the washing-machine 'whizz-kid' in *The Pendulum Years: Britain and the Sixties*. Bloom himself still does not understand what went wrong with his business, although he strews enough clues about in his autobiography *It's No Sin to Make a Profit* (W. H. Allen, 1970). 'Once the rot set in on our sales everything seemed to go wrong for Rolls. But the big question is: why did the rot set in? Even today nobody is certain.' He blames his falling sales in March 1964 on an early spring, because 'housewives do not bother with such things as cookers and vacuum cleaners during the summer months', but goes on to suggest that the main reason for the firm's failure that year was more probably a lack of confidence in the company which had spread to the customers. People were hesitant to buy a Rolls washing machine because if the company failed they would not be able to get after-sales service or spare parts.

There is undoubtedly some truth in this theory, but in all probability the diminution of confidence in the company's products can be traced even further back. Bloom had always sold direct to the housewife and makes no secret of his hostility for the retail trader with his generous mark-up of 30 or 40 per cent, in return for which he claims some professional knowledge of the electrical appliances he sells. Bloom's attitude to the retailer is that he is a parasite and can be cut out without loss to the consumer; indeed the consumer gains greatly in lower selling prices.

He certainly demonstrated that this was true. His machines were noticeably cheaper than those of the established manufacturers and in the long run (he was in the business for about six years) he forced prices in general to come down. According to the spring 1958 issue of *Shopper's Guide* the dominant make was Hoover, with 42 per cent of the market, followed by Hotpoint with 11 per cent, and Bendix with 10 per cent. There were seven other makes on the market with shares ranging from 2 to 9 per cent and fourteen others with less than 1 per cent each. It was a crowded field but if anyone in it was vulnerable it was Hoover which, very likely, was the reason for the initial tie-up between Bloom and Sir Charles Colston, who had left Hoover in 1957 on somewhat uneasy terms (see Case 2).

Looking back to Bloom's beginnings in 1958 one discerns a factor which probably worked in his favour but of which he was completely unaware. *Shopper's Guide* in their survey of the market he was about to enter found that there was a considerable absence of what marketing men call brand loyalty in the cases of Hoover and Goblin. Hoover were selling four types of machine at that time, which accounts to some extent for their strong position, but three of them still had hand or electric wringers instead of spin driers. The Goblin had only a hand wringer. Asked if they would prefer another make nearly half the Hoover owners said yes or that they would prefer the same make with a spin drier. Nearly 60 per cent of Goblin owners replied in this way.

Where the makes did have electric wringers or spin driers there was much more satisfaction and therefore more loyalty to the make. Had anyone been reading this pioneer consumer advice journal with an eye on the market he would have spotted instantly the opening for a cheap 'twin tub' incorporating a spin-drier. The Hoovermatic had recently come on the market but was sufficiently more expensive to discourage owners of the older types of machine from making an immediate changeover, although a large sample of those questioned were intending to go for a twin tub the next time. Enough women in Britain had experienced the advantages of owning a washing machine to be ready to consider an improved version at a relatively low price. Bloom's market was ready-made.

He bought his Electromatic twin tubs in Holland from the Schrouten brothers, advertised them in the *Daily Mirror* at 49 guineas (59 guineas with water heater) and got 8,000 inquiries. 'It was obvious', he says, 'that when people saw how cheap the Electromatic was they suddenly realised that a washing machine was no longer a luxury.' In his rather unsystematic account of the business side of his life he fails to emphasize at this point that one of his selling inducements was that he took old machines in place of a cash deposit (although he later ran into trouble with officialdom for thus circumventing the 'stop-go' hire-purchase rules). He was in fact in the replacement market to quite a large extent.

It is significant that, throughout his book, John Bloom gives little or no consideration to the possibility that his repeated letting down of customers might have contributed in the long run to his financial crisis. His finances had from the outset been based on delays in settlement, whether of purchase tax or of air freight charges or of suppliers' invoices, and when cash flow began to dry up in the early months of 1964 he could not hold out; and the cash had largely flowed from the sales of washing machines.

Delivery delays

Delivery delays were chronic in his early operations. His first advertisements brought in far more orders than he could fill from the Schrouten factory, turning out a hundred a week at the height of its capacity. He turned for additional output to an Italian firm making a good-looking, reliable machine. 'The only trouble was that they did not get people's clothes very clean, so I had to stop selling them. As I had bought a hundred or two, they were a financial disaster I could well have done without.' Disaster is a word used frequently by John Bloom in his book, of his own business operations.

A defecting colleague who set up a rival company deprived Bloom of his Dutch machines at a time when business was building up and he was engaged in negotiating the merger with Rolls Razor which gave him a public quotation for his shares and the name Rolls to tack on to Electromatic. 'The thought of being able to pin the word "Rolls" to my washing machines seemed just too good to be true.' This was ironic at that time because he had to start making his own machines from scratch, buying in most of the parts, using Hoover motors.

This led to even worse delivery delays, to the extent that the newspapers carrying his advertisements (his salesmen were still taking orders and collecting deposits although there were no machines in stock) threatened to stop carrying his announcements. At that stage he needed them more than they needed him (later he became one of the biggest advertising spenders in the country) and to win their confidence he invited the advertising directors to see his factory, which was the Rolls Razor works at Cricklewood. Had he shown them his actual predicament, struggling to make forty machines a week and those of indifferent quality, they would certainly have dropped him and he would have been out of business shortly afterwards. But he chose to deceive them into thinking that his production was in full spate and that scores of machines were being shipped out.

He invited the newspaper executives for a Monday and the week-end was spent arranging an impressive piece of stage management: 'on the Monday of the visit . . . everyone in the factory was bent over some piece of machinery or metal and was wearing a scientific-looking white coat.' The loading bay was apparently choked with finished machines and the assembly line frantically busy, but actually loaded with dismembered old machines being put together again. The loading bay quota represented the previous week's entire output of sixty or so with another ten reassembled during the visit. It worked, and Bloom's advertisements were allowed to continue. 'But that did not solve my other problem—how to produce Rolls Electromatic washing machines that were reliable.'

Not content with replicating the Schrouten design he demanded 'improvements' from his engineers, such as a safety brake on the spin-drier. It was worse than none: 'those early "safety-first" machines used to wobble all over the place in a very dangerous-looking way'. They tried to make the machines empty into the sink by means of a pump, instead of into a bucket on the floor. In May 1960, making 400 machines a week, Rolls Electromatic were 'inundated' with complaints, as the homes of Britain where Bloom machines resided were being inundated with water. 'It seemed as if half the country was spending its time mopping up kitchen floors after trying to empty our machine.'

The September issue of *Which?* records that 'There was pump failure with the first ROLLS and the pump connection worked loose on the second. The spin drier brake tended to jam in the "on" position on this second sample.' But the machine as a whole was far from satisfactory according to this report. Although it was £10 cheaper than any other twin tub (£70. 7*s*. against an average of over £80) 'it did not wash very effectively at the 5 lb. rated load, and even at 3 lb. 6 oz. only moderately well. Its spin drier was about average for the group. The machine might be damaged if the heater was switched on accidentally. The instructions were, we consider, inadequate and the finish only fair.'

Bloom knew he was in trouble with his customers about quality. 'I thought the name of Electromatic was getting such bad publicity that it would be politic to change the name . . .' and he did, to the Starmatic, using a German-made motor 'imported from a respected manufacturer'. They were incorrectly wired (probably because of different wiring conventions) for British use. 'The result was that they were quite literally blowing up in kitchens, giving housewives hysterics, frightening the cat and filling the whole room with swathes of smoke. The Starmatics were being sent back to the factory more quickly than they were going out.'

The 'bad publicity' to which John Bloom refers had been set going by the *Which?* inquiries. He launched the Starmatic in the hope of dodging the criticisms levelled at the Electromatic. *Which?* carried a lengthy footnote on the Starmatic, however, saying that its washing performance seemed much the same and that the spin drier had improved but was liable to corrosion stains 'in a very short time' Evidently their samples had not blown up, but they were still unenthusiastic.

Production at Cricklewood was now 500 a week but lagging behind orders to the extent that Bloom again had anxieties about the press and his precious advertising. The fact that his machines lacked reliability seemed to concern him only marginally, although he now realized that ill-will was accumulating. He refers to this predictable phenomenon mainly in the sense that his competitors, the established manufacturers with their retail outlets, were waiting to savage him for poor quality. Of the housewife he claims that he pursued a policy that she was always right. 'So any woman who had a machine that broke down—and some I'm sorry to say had more than one—always received a replacement.' And the replacements were often no better than the originals. He paid the bills for damaged clothing. 'Whatever happened I made sure that the customer was always happy in the end.' How could he be sure? In 1962 he had sold 101,000 machines, 12 per cent of the market. How many of these customers were dissatisfied but failed to make themselves heard?

The British are notorious for not complaining directly and immediately. Some do, and out of 100,000 even 10 per cent would have kept Bloom's after-sales service department busy. But what of those who put up with their 'bargain' machine and resolved never to touch a Rolls appliance again, and said so to the neighbours? Bloom's ignorance of the pitfalls of manufacturing and selling complex products is revealed in one or two asides in his book. He and Peter Ustinov had discussed taking over the AC car company and selling its distinguished products direct like washing machines. 'Unfortunately we found that there were many problems, the main one being after-sales service, which is essential. I encountered this again when I tried to obtain the selling rights of the little Daf cars.' The implication that after-sales service is a burdensome extra commitment is unavoidable.

So dazzled were some of the businessmen who were not in John Bloom's business, washing machines, that they agreed to tie in with him in the way that Pressed Steel did, giving him control of the refrigerator business, Prestcold. The Pakaway model, which had won a design award, was the star turn at Prestcold at the time. Bloom, on a trip to New York, thought that he should be able to sell it to the big American discount stores. He had already had a brush off from Hambros, the merchant bankers who acted as agents for Austin cars in the United States. They did not see the idea 'as a winner'. With the support of Sir Isaac Wolfson he approached the discount houses with what he calls prototypes, which they were not: 'unfortunately they were not technically 100 per cent and they also fell foul of the regulations of the American Standards Association which were entirely different from British standards'.

This anecdote displays a profound ignorance of the standards system combined with a *naïveté* which prevented Bloom from realizing that in some countries technical performance standards are used as a means of blocking unwanted imports. The Pakaway was, in any case, incurring some criticism on the British market for its inability to take a normal dinner plate on the shelf without, when the door was closed, breaking eggs in the door rack. Not the most scientific of tests but something for the anti-Council of Industrial Design faction to use as ammunition.

His next move in his chosen arena, washing machines, he describes as 'a first-class piece of long-term planning' which 'blew up in my face'. This forecast was that the automatic washing machine would eventually displace the twin tub and that Rolls should be ready with a model; one with an action that could dry as a spin drier could, which was as cheap as a twin tub and light enough to be carried about by the salesman. His colleague Irving Jacobs claimed to have made such a prototype in 1962 but refused to reveal the secret of his suspension, which he had patented, unless he were paid royalties. He had set up the Washing Machine Research and Development Company for the purpose, unknown to Bloom. It cost Pressed Steel

£110,000 for tooling and £16,000 in royalties, but the automatic never went into production 'because of various technical difficulties', not to mention a split with the Pressed Steel management.

Meanwhile Rolls twin tubs were selling under the names of Rapide de luxe, which had replaced the Starmatic, and Concorde de luxe which replaced the Rapide, once again on the eve of a *Which?* report. This report referred to both models as similar, pointing out the misleading nature of the Rolls advertisements which failed to mention that the 39-guinea Rapide was without a heater. At this time Bloom was showering his customers with free gifts, and *Which?* pointed this out, adding that buyers could also receive 5,000 of Bloom's own Supa Golden trading stamps with a cash value of £2 or more if they accepted gifts. All this and an advertising budget for 1963 of £1,720,000 sold 201,400 machines, 19·7 per cent of the market, bringing Rolls up to second place to Hoover. Bloom's salesmen were selling as many as 7,000 machines a week and earning £100 in commissions. They received no salaries or fringe benefits and worked under constant and even sinister pressure from Jack Jacobs, Irving's brother, who would obliquely threaten backsliding salesmen with the sack.

It was very hard selling, with no attention to customer satisfaction in the long term if at all. At least not satisfaction with the product, rather with the bargain in all its glory of premium offers and other inducements. Bloom came under fire from *Which?* for his high hire-purchase charges, amounting to a real rate of interest of over 20 per cent per annum as against under 10 from most other firms. He dismisses this as having been out of his hands, but it cannot have redounded to his credit.

Double your money?

He had by the end of 1963 been trading for five full years and doubling his sales each year. As long as sales continued to rise the advertising and premium offer cost per sale could be kept within bounds, even while the individual offer was made increasingly more generous. It made sense to Bloom that by doubling this expenditure in 1964 he could double his sales to 400,000 units and come closer to ousting Hoover as market leader. He set his advertising appropriation at an unprecedented £3 million, 'spurred on by the 25,003 machines I sold in October—but the monthly total never again reached even 20,000.

On advertising alone therefore I began paying out twice as much as was warranted by sales.'

Clearly there was more to Bloom's downfall than the failure of his attempt to monopolize the washing machine market. Most of his diversification ventures were ill-advised and futile. His foray into trading stamps using the products of Great Universal Stores for redemption 'turned out to be a disastrous move'. And there were others. No doubt if the washing machines had continued to bring in the revenue he could have survived some of his 'disasters' but they did not. Pressed Steel could not keep the unit cost of the machines they were making down to his figure of £23 and gave notice early in 1963, whereupon Bloom tried to switch production to Sir Charles Colston's Tallent Engineering. The former Hoover managing director had long since set up his Colston Appliances firm to sell the dishwasher (Case 2).

In the background was his Bulgarian holiday fiasco, which had also failed to meet its target of 8,000 bookings for the summer of 1963, as agreed with the Sofia government, and had incurred some adverse press publicity because of the poor conditions under which some of the holidaymakers were transported and lodged. These holidays were also used as a selling inducement for both salesmen and customers. The man who had convinced Bloom originally of the potentialities of Bulgarian packaged holidays, Bertie Littman, was concerned that the first planeloads of holidaymakers consisted of Rolls salesmen and their families taking their rewards for successful selling. This too well-known operation and the public break with the respected Pressed Steel may have helped to bring down the Bloom empire. But the foundation, washing machines, showed distinct signs of giving way before the end of 1963. Early in 1964 a rapid decline in sales set in, pushing the promotional cost of a machine up from over £9 in January to £14 plus in March, not to mention the £5 worth of premiums. Regardless of the manufacturing costs in 1964, about £20 at least, a Rolls Concorde selling at £40. 19*s.* without heater would have cost nearly half that to sell. In other words by the spring of 1964 Bloom was only breaking even on his cheap machines without counting overheads and barely making a net profit on the better models. Apparently he was unaware of this at the time, although he gives the figures in his book.

When the production costs, promotional and commission costs, and overheads are all estimated it seems that by March or April 1964,

Rolls might have been taking a loss on every machine sold. Whether sales were falling or not, and they certainly were, from 19,452 in January to 19,238 in February to a catastrophic 16,104 in March, the company was bound to be in severe financial trouble. Bloom had budgeted for a monthly average sale of 32,000 based on 1963 actual sales figures rather arbitrarily projected into 1964 as capable of being doubled by means of doubling promotional spending, as crude a piece of marketing as could be conceived.

We have seen that the Rolls Electromatic venture came to full fruition at a time when the washing machine market was about to undergo some changes, first by means of the switch to twin tubs, later because of the launching of the big automatics. The centre of the market was the twin tub, and it was here that the biggest sales expansion took place in the early 1960s, boosting the ownership figures from under 40 per cent by households to over 60. Rolls undoubtedly took more than their share of this growth by the direct selling method, with its advantages of cheapness, in a price elastic situation, but also of dynamism. The Rolls philosophy, if it can be dignified by such a term, was to establish a conversion ratio of 2 to 1: for every two serious inquiries a definite sale, and the sales force was under pressure to hit this target. The relatively passive selling of the former market leaders, advertising, selling through shops and show-rooms, with the sales force selling to the retailer, and costly after-sales service, could not withstand this onslaught in the short run.

From reading Bloom's own account of these years, and there are some interesting omissions from the business record (such as the actual percentage of complaints and rejects at any time), one could be led to believe as he does that his downfall was the consequence of united opposition by his competitors, who preferred the security of dealer selling to the unpredictable rough and tumble of direct selling. He evidently formed a personal dislike for Arthur Earle, Colston's successor as managing director of Hoover, who 'provoked' him by announcing that in contrast to the one-product direct-selling firms Hoover were able to diversify into such items as fan heaters. He announced this at the October 1963 sales conference of his company. Bloom discovered that the heater was made under license from Solartron, a member of the Firth Cleveland group, took out a licence, and had a heater designed to be a replica of the Hoover 3000, naming it Rolls 3333, 'provocatively'. But he planned to give it away, to the tune of 50,000 or 60,000, mainly to damage the sales of the 14-guinea

Hoover appliance. He was delighted to get this extravagant gesture into a BBC radio news bulletin. No wonder that the sales figure for the week before the Rolls national conference in the autumn of 1963 'came to a staggering 7,442' with salesmen taking home commissions of £100. But at what cost had those sales been obtained? And just how repeatable was the achievement in the absence of yet more extravagant 'free offers'?

No such questions seem to have occurred to the senior management of the Rolls company. But Bloom knew that the name of Rolls was accumulating ill-will (the infamous hire-purchase terms were making more profit than the machines themselves, he admits) and was in the course of dropping it altogether when the firm crashed. His eleventh-hour scheme was to switch out of Rolls into Tallent, with the Tallentwin, virtually the same machine but with less promotion expenditure and therefore a slightly lower selling price: 3 guineas below the Concorde.

It was a flop, mainly, thinks Bloom, because of the small promotion budget. The next thing was talks with Duomatic, the company launched by the defecting colleague who had hived off the Schrouten output. When these failed Bloom made a bid to get into the fully automatic market by buying Zanussi machines off Imperial Domestic Appliances, who were selling them direct. To make a profit Rolls had to sell them more cheaply than Imperial: 'even with this disadvantage I decided that I could still offer an automatic at less than the Imperial price by cutting on the finish and the speed of action, and by substituting a 1½ kw heater for the 3 kw'. Thus was the Rolls Robot born. The de luxe version was identical with the Imperial. The firm was in the run down to insolvency at this time, so even the desperate cost-cutting was of no use. It is worth adding to the account because of the evident disregard for quality when profits were at stake.

The rest of the story is of last-minute bids to rescue an operation which had over the years condemned itself. If there is any marketing lesson to be learnt from the Rolls Electromatic story it is that in the long run, and five years is not all that long compared with Hoover who have been in operation in this country since 1919, it does not pay to bilk the customer. Lavish selling baits and pushful if not hard selling work only as long as the goods show themselves good. In real life quality and reliability are seldom found hand in hand with showmanship; at least not on the business scene, or not for long.

CASE

8 *Giving 'em socks*

Not a very exciting commodity, the sock. Sales are steady rather than scintillating, so steady in fact, even in the United States where all markets are supposed to be dynamic, that the US National Association of Hosiery Manufacturers retained the services of Dr Ernest Dichter to find means of stimulating them into a rising trend.

According to a report in the *International Herald Tribune* in the summer of 1970 the good doctor's report, *Soxology: A Strategy for Stimulating Sock Sales*, might or might not have been a satire. They certainly had a lot of fun with it, anyway. 'Some of it', said columnist Russell Baker, 'appears to have been written by Art Buchwald.' Buchwald has been for many years one of the *Trib.*'s leading humorists. Dichter had said such things as 'an empty sock drawer is a symbol of an empty heart', and 'the sock user should be reminded . . . that while he has a close attachment to his socks, he doesn't love all of them equally'.

More significantly for marketing men, Dichter also commented that: 'There is not enough obsolescence, not enough pride in their possession.' It was the second part of that sentence, obsolescence by fashion change, on which the Dichter report concentrated. Socks, especially if made of pure wool, have a natural obsolescence. They wear out. Partly for reasons of washing convenience, partly because of the rising cost of wool and the relative cheapness of man-made fibres, but also as a means of appealing to wives weary of the darning needle, it has become almost universal to manufacture socks from blends of natural and man-made fibres or to make them entirely of synthetic yarns.

It is strange but true that in its sixteen years of existence *Which?* has never surveyed men's socks on behalf of its reader-members. *Shopper's Guide*, which ceased publication when the Consumer Council and its journal *Focus* replaced the British Standard Institution's Consumer Advisory Council in 1966, dealt with socks in its sixth issue, autumn 1968. It described all the main materials from which socks were knitted at that time, including spun nylon, but failed to mention a brand of spun nylon sock that had by then been on the British market for at least six years.

This omission was an interesting one for the simple reason that among the qualities tabulated by the researchers on p. 25 of that issue of the Guide was listed durability, alongside warmth, elasticity, and absorption. Nylon scored by far the highest for durability, but did badly in the other three tests, the spun variety scoring even lower than the stretch yarn.

Spun nylon is made by taking continuous filament nylon, chopping it up into staple lengths to resemble the staple fibres of wool, and spinning the fibres into a yarn that has a superficial resemblance to real wool. According to *Shopper's Guide*, however, the socks which they tested, that had been knitted from such wool-like yarn, had not acquired the desirable characteristics of wool: warmth and absorbency. But in their comments on the performance of stretch nylon socks they lamented the fact that they had been unable to find a thick nylon sock to test, because they believed that such a sock would probably have all the necessary qualities and be very long-lasting.

They were quite right. The missing brand happened to be worn by a journalist, a member of the team contributing to the Consuming Interest column of *The Spectator*, under the pseudonym of Leslie Adrian. In the issue of 20 April 1962 he referred to Essinay socks as capable of lasting ten years without wearing into holes, even though they did pill (form small balls of fibre on the surface), felted on the sole and therefore shrunk a little, and they did discolour. But they never wore into holes, and they were warm and absorbent.

This revelation triggered off a spurt of interest in the sock and the author received a letter from the makers, Simpson, Wright and Lowe Ltd of Sutton-in-Ashfield, Nottinghamshire, thanking him for having stimulated thirty-two inquiries for the now celebrated sock. Not long after this correspondence with Mr J. W. Elder, a director of the small and rather obscure firm, the writer began to receive letters from *Spectator* readers complaining that they could not buy the socks in their locality.

No doubt those who had written direct to the makers had either been sent their orders or had been referred to an appropriate retailer. But there were numbers of others who simply went round to their nearest outfitters and asked for Essinay socks. Some of them received a cold negative, followed up with the explanation that because the socks lasted so long there was too little profit in them to make it worth while to stock them.

Alarmed by this news the journalist, living in London, hastened to a department store in Oxford Street and demanded several pairs of the controversial socks. After some casting about a box was found under the counter and a few pairs in the correct size were purchased. That was the last time that individual was able to buy the Essinay brand. It has now disappeared from the market altogether.

In order to compile this brief chapter the author wrote to Simpson, Wright and Lowe and received from the chief accountant the news that not only was nobody connected with the old Essinay brand still with the firm, but also that the entire management had changed and it was impossible to disinter any information as to the fate of the long-life sock and its innovators or even to pass a message to the members of the former board of directors, all of them having apparently disappeared leaving no trace of their existence.

There have been many rumours over the years that big business, anxious to profit by obsolescence, will buy up and suppress any innovation, such as an everlasting match, that threatens to slow down the process of consumption and rapid replacement. So far there has never been any concrete evidence that such action was ever taken. The cigarette lighter must have prevented the consumption of countless matches but does not seem to have suffered from any attempt by the match-makers to keep it off the market.

The Essinay sock, which did last too long and did interfere with the preferred process of obsolescence and wear and tear, in a rather restricted and humble area of consumption it is true, was not obliterated by the machinations of big business. The market for socks is hardly that important. The really interesting thing about the Essinay story is that the distributive system refused to support the brand.

At first there was a measure of enthusiasm for the idea of selling even a small garment that had such a unique selling proposition, and the initial price was high at 11*s*. a pair in 1952. But when the price came down nearer to the average for a pair of socks, say 7*s*. at the time (1960–2), the margin of profit was too small for the retailer, who knew that repeat sales would be spaced out infinitely longer than for less durable wares. Gradually, therefore, retail orders to Sutton-in-Ashfield dried up. Depending upon the retail trade and not selling direct by mail-order the company either had to drop the line or go out of business. Whichever happened first we do not know. We do know that here is a real-life example of a durable product which the public evidently wanted but which, for reasons of profitability on the part of the distributors, they could not be allowed to have. Marketing men will not need to have the lesson spelled out.

The consumer

There are two persistent myths about consumption in a market economy. The first is that, given an unrestricted pricing system, the consumer is 'sovereign', that is to say that it is consumer spending which ultimately governs what shall be produced and sold. The other myth is the twin one of consumer rationality and holds that consumer choice is 'rational', meaning that the decision to buy is based on a considered choice which must, in its turn, be guided by adequate if not complete knowledge.

Neither of these stands up to close scrutiny, although both have enjoyed a long run in the elementary economics textbooks, having their origins in orthodox micro-economics. One dictionary of economics has rightly labelled consumer sovereignty as naïve,[1] the concept being an oversimplification based on the classic demand and supply model of a 'perfect' market. In this abstract model no account is taken of advertising and other sales pressures. It is presumed that a price is given, and that it is a price which equates demand with supply. When the two are exactly equal, at the point where the demand and supply curves intersect with the price line (which is a straight line parallel to the horizontal ordinates because the price under these conditions is unchanging), the system is said to be in equilibrium.

Changes in demand, up or down, will not affect the price unless the supply cannot expand or contract correspondingly (a circumstance not admitted in this particular model), but will bring about supply changes sufficient to restore the equilibrium. This familiar elementary statement has its uses in the development of economic theory but cannot be expected to apply, except in very special conditions, to the reality of commerce. To declare on this basis, therefore,

1. Taylor, P. A. S., *A New Dictionary of Economics* (Routledge & Kegan Paul, 1966), p. 43.

that the dynamic force in the demand–supply relationship is demand is less than naïve, it is untrue.

The perfect market of the demand–supply model is one in which every would-be buyer and every seller has complete knowledge of every other and of the goods that they are offering for sale or exchange. This *ignis fatuus* of abstract economics was actually pursued in the Middle Ages under the name of 'market overt' or the open market. Elaborate rules and controls were devised to try to ensure that all goods for sale in a market were actually 'pitched', that is exposed to the scrutiny of buyers and other sellers. No 'examples' or samples were permitted. The intention was for buyers to be able to make thorough comparisons of all similar goods on offer, the ultimate object being that all bargains struck would be at prices approximating to another ideal, the 'just' price.[1]

In such a setting of open trading it is little wonder that the doctrine *caveat emptor*, putting the onus on the buyer, should prevail. It would certainly have seemed that the buyer was in a strong position, being able to inspect all that was for sale of a particular class of goods, and to pick and choose. In reality it was not so simple, and the authorities who controlled markets waged a constant battle to see that the law of market overt was observed, which means that in practice it was constantly being flouted. This is not the place to go into detail as to the manner in which the traditional defences of the individual were gradually eroded, so that ultimately he ceased to be in touch with the producers of the goods he bought, and dealt mainly with middlemen. But it must be observed that the longer the chain of distribution becomes, the more difficult it is for the producer to keep in touch with the consumer and the more both come to rely on the intervening merchants, the one for outlets, the other for purchases. It follows that the men in the middle, while naturally keen to make sales, will tend to have their own interests at heart and not those of the other two parties.

Consumer protection

Consumer protection, or whatever we choose to call it, is not then entirely the result of technological advance and the consequent complexity of goods in the third quarter of the twentieth century. It springs

1. See, for example, Robertson, A. B., 'The open market in the city of London in the eighteenth century', *East London Papers*, 1, 2.

originally from the recognition that the seller almost always has the whip hand. It is one thing, however, to defend the buyer of food and clothing against the stronger bargaining power and even the deviousness of the seller, whether he be producer or not. Protection becomes much more necessary when the goods are no longer as simple to evaluate as meat and bread, woollen cloth, leather footwear, and beer, all of which it was assumed (wrongly as it turned out) could be assessed for quality in the light of experience and natural observation.

What may a consumer be expected to know of plastics wares, pharmaceuticals, electronic devices, electrical appliances, processed foods, and man-made fibres and their blends? Both the consumer and the manufacturer, not to mention the intermediate dealers, are aware of the balance of knowledge; that it is bound to favour the maker. There has, therefore, to be some trust placed in the maker by the purchaser, and there are numerous examples of such confidence being justified. Unfortunately there are as many to illustrate the opposite, not all of them instances of deliberate deception, technological complexity having on occasions been underestimated by the manufacturer as a possible obstacle to consumer acceptance.

The outstanding case to be documented on this point is that of the Ford Edsel, of which *Consumer Reports*, journal of the Consumers' Union of the United States, remarked in 1958: 'more uselessly overpowered, more gadget bedecked, more hung with expensive accessories than any car in its price class'. Another comment (both come from John Brooks's *Business Adventures* [Gollancz, 1969]) was that: 'To look at the Edsel buttons pulls the driver's eyes clear off the road. The "luxury-loaded Edsel"—as one magazine cover described it—will certainly please anyone who confuses gadgetry with true luxury.'

Complexity may not have been the only or even the main reason for public rejection of the Edsel models, but it was undoubtedly one of them and appears to have arisen from the results of a market research survey which inquired of a large sample of American car owners what they would wish to find in their ideal car. This is rather like putting the hoary old question to men about their ideal woman. The resultant 'model' is nonexistent in nature. But when the Ford executives and engineers saw the analysis of the ideal motor car they went ahead and built it. The result seems to have encountered the reception accorded proverbially to people who try to be all things to all men.

It is significant in this connection that Brooks records the disgust of the Ford executives who watched the spurning of their ideal automobile with the simultaneous acceptance of the Volkswagen.

People weren't in the mood for the Edsel. Why not is a mystery to me. What they'd been buying for several years encouraged the industry to build exactly this kind of car. We gave it to them, and they wouldn't take it. Well, they shouldn't have acted like that. You can't just wake up somebody one day and say, 'That's enough, you've been running in the wrong direction.' Anyway, *why* did they do it? Golly, the industry worked and worked over the years—getting rid of gear shifting, providing interior comfort, providing plus performance for use in emergencies! And now the public wants these little beetles. I don't get it!

This candid outburst might almost serve as a sample reaction by business managers everywhere to the apathy of consumers in the face of what they themselves would call a 'breakthrough', 'an engineering marvel', 'an unparalleled advance', etc., etc. When it comes to failure, is it the customer who is always wrong? That would be a most unwise conclusion, but not unknown in the motor industry as was observed in Case 1.

Professor Theodore Levitt has commented (in *Innovation in Marketing* [Pan Piper, 1962]) that 'Most businesses and most sellers think they do a pretty good job of marketing, of discovering, of taking care of the customer's complex needs.' But, he goes on, in spite of (or because of?) all the information so eagerly and assiduously assembled 'this seldom produces any really solid advances in the creation of consumer satisfaction . . .' And he concludes that the chief reason for this shortcoming is that 'neither the researchers nor the corporate bosses know what they are really trying to do'. We have observed that, too often, the 'corporate bosses' are isolated from their consuming public.

But the market researchers seem to know what they are trying to do. Their aim is to inform their clients, those same corporate bosses, about marketing opportunities in such a way that they are able to maximize their sales. The corporate bosses, it has been assumed in the orthodox theory of the firm, maximize sales in order to maximize revenue and profits with a view to future growth.

For our purpose it is unnecessary to enter into the argument as to whether large corporations attempt to maximize their profits or not (the more recent exponents of theory of the firm contend that profit margins are optimized, that is that the corporate manager aims at a satisfactory profit for the shareholders and not at the largest possible net revenue he can make. The neologism for this is 'satisficing'!). In dealing with consumer satisfaction the earning of long-term profit is the reward for creating that satisfaction. The problem here is the creation of that satisfaction, which on the face of it looks like a restoration of consumer sovereignty. In fact it is not.

Consumer sovereignty remains an acceptable myth, although it is a concept based on an untenable assumption, which is that all goods and services are brought into being in obedience to the consumer's expressed preferences, expressed in the form of purchasing power. We know, however, that manufacturers continually disappoint the consumer in a number of ways and when they do, as with the Ford executive and the response to the Edsel, tend to put the blame not on themselves but on the customer. Case 1 illustrated this point amply enough.

The old concept of consumer sovereignty therefore contains an inherent contradiction, that goods and services are produced and offered in response to the consumer's express demand, but that when he or she rejects them it is not the producer's fault for failing to meet the consumer's needs but the consumer's fault for failing to perceive the excellence of the offering. Surely if business people really believed in consumer sovereignty in its original conception they would succeed more often in pleasing the consumer?

On the whole it would be better to dispense with this awkward concept of sovereignty and concentrate instead on the simpler idea of satisfaction. This has the advantage that it can be looked at from the point of view of producing goods and services that match the consumer's expectations both in terms of the seller's claims, that is that they are fit for the purpose intended and stated, and also in terms of efficiency, that is to say not over-complicated nor of an unnecessarily high quality.

If the eight cases in this book are looked at in this way we can see that the Vauxhall Viva did not come up to expectations in the eyes of quite a large sample of customers; that the Colston dishwasher, while perfectly apt for its purpose, fulfilled a function not wanted by enough customers; that freeze-dried food similarly lacks appropriateness for a large number of people; that *London Life* was aimed at a group of consumers who evidently do not read magazines or at any rate not much; that a smokeless briquette was certainly needed but proved to be technologically too costly; that Corfam turned out not to be a mass production commodity; that even direct selling and heavy advertising cannot sell an appliance which has lost its reputation for reliability; and that in our distribution system even if customer satisfaction is achieved, as with the Essinay sock, you have to please the retailer too, or cut him out.

Variety reduction

That it is possible to home in more accurately on the consumer as a business target was made clear in an example cited by Sir Frederick Catherwood, former Director-General of the National Economic Development Office in one of his speeches. The appropriate Economic Development Committee, or 'little Neddy', had been questioning a firm of manufacturers of ladies' foundation garments about their high production cost problem and how to solve it. One of their criticisms was that the garments were catalogued in too many subtle shades of pink or flesh colour, as many as 30 or 40. Could not the variety be reduced, asked the experts? No, replied the manufacturers, over a long time they had learnt that this was the range of shades that the market demanded.

With the firm's permission an investigation into sales according to colour was made, with the predictable discovery that 80 per cent of the firm's sales came from two or three of the shades and none at all from a significant number. No doubt, variety reduction would lose the firm some marginal sales, but evidently no one had asked at what cost those sales were obtained.

Here was a firm treating the consumer as sovereign in a way that could benefit neither party. As to the rationality of choice, in the case of such colour differences, discernible only at wide shade intervals, there could be little or none. Above all, the intention of the management was to satisfy the assumed preferences of its customers. This was not a large, complex company, of the size and type which fashionably bears the blame for being out of touch with markets. It was just another company, small to medium-sized by conventional measurements, imprisoned in its own experience and apparently unable to break out without outside help.

Sustaining this manufacturer in his high cost error was no doubt the conviction that he was 'giving the public what it wanted', without ever finding out whether he was doing so in reality. The other side of this coin is that frequently manufacturers do the opposite of the corset-maker, they cut out lines arbitrarily leaving their erstwhile customers hunting around for their favourite product. This is illustrated by the old cynical jibe about the shop assistant who said to a persistent customer, 'I've already told you, and you're the twelfth person this morning, that there's no call for that brand.'

There is an important problem in choosing between the single standard product (the Model T Ford in black only or its modern counterpart the Volkswagen, in a range of colours) and the fullest possible range of styles, colours, and prices (which in its extreme version has become known in the motor industry as 'badge engineering' because of its sheer superficiality). Too much monotony or too much variety are to be avoided, obviously, but there are products in which monotony is acceptable, like cheap ball-point pens. Too much variety is always going to cost too much, while at the same time making less impact on the market than a smaller, better-chosen range. It should not be beyond the ability of the smallest company to keep a running assessment of sales from a range of styles or models and gradually to contract the range to the measurable optimum. But how often is it done? Can it be that too many manufacturers believe that unnecessary variety raises sales? And does it? It can never do any harm to find out, as the corset maker was prompted into doing, just how on target your product line is. It is worth reiterating that you can miss your consumer target just as easily by trying too hard as by not trying hard enough.

It is at this point that a reference back to the introduction reminds us that a little reality is now being injected into that other myth, consumer rationality. It was, of course, convenient and tidy to team the two, sovereignty and rationality, together. Such a formidable combination helped to lend reality to the concept of the perfect market, demand, supply, and price equilibrium and marginal analysis. We then have an ideal situation, with economic man in a dominant position in the market and capable of rational, that is knowledgeable, choice. As a theoretical construction for purposes of development into more subtle and less abstract forms there is little we need say about it here.

As a picture of the market faced by the average business it has little or no value. But some rationality is creeping in, with the aid of legislation, consumer protection, and comparative testing, and it would be unwise to ignore it and pointless to try to prevent it. As we have already remarked in the introduction, a better strategy would be to make the fullest possible use of the apparatus so presented, in order to arrive at a closer understanding of the modern consumer. Let us remember Dichter's wise words, that the consumer does not like to feel that he has been foolish in his choice, that he has been in any way trapped into a purchase, or tricked into signing some agreement or warranty which undermines his rights as a buyer.

As industrial society increases in affluence the number of consumers likely not only to react in this way but to take some action about it is going to grow. Such disappointment is liable to generate a fairly vigorous reaction against the product, at least among the AB group of consumers. There is some indication that this kind of response disappears further down the income scale from C1 to E, which is doubtless why the less subtle forms of persuasion are directed at the lower income groups—and the lower age-groups too, for other, more obvious reasons.

One commentator has said, however, that heavy advertising expenditure has begun to show 'a truly counter-productive pay-off. If a system claims daily and nightly that a series of products are what they are not, a point is reached when no statement is believed. For many recipients, an automatic negative effect occurs, or the statement is blotted out altogether.'[1] In a footnote this writer added that not all advertisers follow this policy, and that some of the most successful are scrupulously 'factual' in their advertising. (His quotation marks.)

All of this is by way of sounding a warning note against the danger of marketing arrogance *vis-à-vis* the consumer, and coming to look upon one's fellow men as so many statistics on so many charts, to be manoeuvred here and there like molecules in a chemical reaction. Chemists know how far they can go in shuffling the 'building blocks' of materials about in order to make other materials, but even they get unexpected results, sometimes total failures and occasional explosions. Is marketing so much more scientific than chemistry?

If these remarks sound wildly irrelevant to the reader, a few examples may suffice in illustration of their application to quite a large area of commerce, an area dominated by marketing mystique. There are certain commodities which lend themselves particularly well to that exercise which is familiar to economists under the name of product differentiation. Washing powders, pet foods, cosmetics, hard and soft drinks, processed foods of most kinds, uniform products

1. Bowen, Ian, *Acceptable Inequalities* (Allen & Unwin, 1970), p. 27.

like nylon stockings, pharmaceuticals, cigarettes, domestic appliances of certain kinds, and numerous other categories. What all these have in common is that it is possible to present several versions of the same product, or one basically the same but superficially different, as in some way significantly different.

What differences there are between, say, toilet soaps, are then 'branded' upon the product. Examples are to be found everywhere. In toilet soap (where variations may take the form of shape, scent, colour, packaging, name, and so on, but it is still soap) the unique selling proposition (USP) is often unreal, taking the form of cosmetic properties, deodorant potential, health-giving qualities, and the like. Commonsense should tell the user that all these benefits would, if they were real, be common to all soaps. The battle for the customer's attention, money, and loyalty is therefore a mock battle, waged with all those weapons for the use of which the advertising industry has so often been criticized: sex appeal, fear, social insecurity, the whole gamut of psychological bullying. It is, in short, manipulation.

It is not the purpose of this chapter to denounce these practices. As far as they go, they have shown themselves to have some commercial advantages, although it was a chairman of Unilever, Lord Heyworth, who said that his company knew that half its advertising was wasted, the trouble was that they did not know which half. That there is an element of waste in this kind of advertising has been strongly urged a number of times (see for a recent example, E. J. Mishan's *Twenty-one Popular Economic Fallacies*, Chapter 9, 'Expenditure on Commercial Advertising is Warranted'). Marketing managers are uneasily aware of this, too, but it is the living of the agencies that is at stake here and a strong lobby in favour of advertising of any kind naturally pushes the contrary arguments.

In product innovation, however, advertising and its peripheral activities, such as so-called press relations or 'product publicity', can sometimes be a trap. By relying too much on these methods of attracting and increasing sales, manufacturers may be in danger of neglecting the intrinsic qualities of the product which will ensure lasting public appreciation and long-term profits. Ford are said to have lost $350 million on the Edsel, and their advertising agency, Foote, Cone, and Belding, also lost money, having opened a new office with a staff of sixty specially to push that model. No amount of publicity could save that product from eventual rejection, and it is by no means an isolated instance. How could it be in a business where eight or nine products out of ten fail to survive?

It would seem that in this chapter an argument has been advanced that favours the use of manipulative techniques, because the consumer lacks the rationality to discriminate between products on grounds of intrinsic quality, price, and other tangible attributes. If that is the inference that the reader draws he should read the case-histories again. The marketing mix, as the professionals like to call it, is not the panacea it once was. Perhaps it never really was, except for somewhat bogus products that needed an 'image' because they had nothing else.

It is increasingly likely that in the future it will become even less of a panacea. Not only are the organized consumer groups growing (the Consumers' Association now has over 600,000 members and shows signs of reaching a million in the next few years) but also the statutory limitations are on the increase, hedging the marketeer round even more closely with regulations about descriptions, labels (no pretty pictures of strawberries on a totally synthetic food, for example), advertising claims, and even the manner in which the advertising is conducted. So while the individual consumer may not be the rational picker and chooser of micro-economic abstraction, collectively he is able to achieve a level of information that can put him increasingly closer to that ideal state. At the same time, officialdom is becoming more and more his ally by cutting back the undergrowth of claims and counter-claims, half-truths and untruths that has for too long obscured the true worth, if any, of too many products.

There is the imminent possibility that the consumer will indeed become sovereign, although in a rather different form from that conceived by the classical economists. This change will not be sudden. It is bound to be gradual, even insidious from the point of view of the marketing executive striving to avoid the numerous pitfalls. But it has already begun. The relatively trivial fines for breaches of the already complex law (the literature on consumer law is already voluminous, as may be seen from the bibliography) may not be a deterrent. The true importance of this transformation of the marketing scene lies rather in the long-range impact on a firm's business of public awareness of the reality behind the marketing smokescreen, if such it is.

Conclusion

Most of the case-histories in this small book have dealt with failure or qualified success, in terms of the market place. The selection has been random, though not entirely, and its scope has been somewhat limited by shortage of time and other resources. Nevertheless assiduous readers who have not found themselves either too depressed or too hostile to persevere will have picked up one message at least.

In his recent book *The Age of Discontinuity* (Heinemann, 1969), Peter Drucker cited the parallel cases of Edison and Swan, who both invented versions of the incandescent lamp. Of them he said:

> The best technical work on the electric light bulb was done not by Edison but by his British competitor, Sir Joseph Swan. And yet it was Edison's bulb that won out in the market-place—for the simple reason that, unlike Swan, Edison looked at the market. He put himself into the position of the electric power companies and asked: 'What do they need and what can they use?' And he put himself in the position of the home owner and asked much the same questions. Technically Swan's solution may have been much more elegant; but it just did not fit the expectations, the behaviour, the values of the two markets which had to accept the new product if it was to be economically possible, let alone successful [p. 48].

The message may be made to seem too facile; that it is a basic error to look upon any new product (as opposed to a 'new' one which is riding on the back of a previous success to begin with) as in any way automatically acceptable once certain marketing rituals have been observed. Yet this assumption is made all the time by manufacturing companies, stimulated by a good idea, a success in the laboratory or, to quote Robert Oppenheimer, the 'technical sweetness' of a new product or process.

The 'elegance' of Swan's incandescent lamp was not sufficient on its own to win the interest and support of the electricity suppliers and the electricity consumers. Emerson has been credited with the claim that 'If a man write a better book, preach a better sermon, or make a better mousetrap than his neighbour, tho' he build his house in the woods, the world will make a beaten path to his door'. It is this cosy assumption that the better mousetrap is bound to win over all other mousetraps that contains the hazardous philosophy: if the product is good it is bound to sell.

But good for what? We have seen that it can, in some respects, be 'too good', like Corfam for some sectors of its intended market. This is not as easily recognized as the situation when the product is not good enough (as we have also seen, this is frequently a deliberate business decision, where it would be nonsense for the opposite to be).

There is an actual instance of a better mousetrap being marketed in the United States and failing, not because it was too expensive, although it cost 7 cents against 3 cents for the familiar wire and wood throwaway affair, but because it was elegantly designed for repeat use but in fact few people like to extract the dead mouse and reuse the lethal apparatus. They prefer the cheaper trap and to discard trap and victim together, suitably shrouded in tissue. In this case can it be said that the more expensive gadget was in fact 'better'? Better in marketing means more satisfactory for the customer.

At this point in our reasoning we find ourselves talking marketing and production talk simultaneously, which is something that most books on marketing and most books on production, not to mention most books on management, fail to do. Typically, marketing writers concentrate on selling, production writers on the technicalities of manufacture and production control. They reflect the preoccupations of their specialist readers. Texts for general management will enshrine all aspects of business management including these (for example, E. F. L. Brech's monumental *The Principles and Practice of Management*, over 1,000 pages in the second edition of 1963), but with seldom a mention of innovation.

Marketing writers often discuss new product introduction. Colin McIver's *Marketing*, which bears the copyright of the Institute of Practitioners in Advertising, goes so far as to discuss why so many new products fail. He gives five reasons: a poor product; a straight, unoriginal imitation; failure to estimate a market; poor customer acceptance; hasty launching to beat a competitor to the market. The most common reason in his experience is 'the natural enthusiasm of all concerned to take a product forward even on the slimmest possibility of ultimate profit' (Pan Books, 1968, pp. 189–90).

If you examine all six explanations together, and they are commonly advanced in connection with new product failure, you find that they are all connected. The enthusiasm of the producers, who are traditionally supposed to have dominated British industry at the expense of marketing success, leads them to rush into innovation when convinced that the idea is promising, spurred on by the threat of being overtaken by competitors.

The poor product or unoriginal product does not happen this way (it all depends what is meant by 'poor': poor quality or inappropriateness), but they are still off target, which is the customer. 'Poor customer acceptance' is at the root of most unsuccessful product innovation, whether the reason is poor quality, high price (high cost), over-complexity (the 'Edsel factor'), lack of 'need' or eventual disappointment with an initially 'satisfactory' product.

In industrial innovation, which may be defined briefly as the introduction of new products or processes for the use of industrial organizations, the discipline is severer than in consumer product innovation, for the obvious reason that the institutional customer is far better equipped to criticize than the individual shopper. The contrast has been well brought out by Eirlys Roberts in her little book *Consumers* (Watts, 1966). She reveals the origins of the American 'consumer movement', the Consumers' Research and the Consumers' Union organizations, which arose between the wars on the initiative of two former employees of the American Standards Association, Schlink and Kallet. They had observed how the Army tested products before purchase and found that they could bulk buy cheaper, superior products to those offered to the private citizen.

The reason was not simply the one that immediately springs to mind, that bulk buying is cheaper. It was testing that mattered, something that the shopper cannot do. True, the price difference between single purchases and bulk or wholesale is to be expected, but not of the order of ten or twenty times as much for the retail article. Nor can the price discrepancy between, say, rice at 7 cents a pound and 'puffed rice' at 61 cents a pound or between wheat at 2½ cents a pound and 'puffed wheat' at 68 cents a pound be explained in terms of costs and 'reasonable profit'. The American investigators satisfied themselves that large sections of the public were being deceived and set about the task of undeceiving them by publishing to subscribers analyses of food and drink, comparative tests of appliances and other information of a kind likely to restore a measure of the lost consumer sovereignty.

We argued earlier that in all probability there never were many cases of true consumer sovereignty, hence the formulation of the medieval concept of *caveat emptor*, which was all very well at a time when commodities were few and simple. Once life became at all complex, especially with the disappearance of the open market, it was difficult for the buyer to beware. Frederick Accum, the analytical chemist, published his *Treatise on the Adulteration of Food, and Culinary Poisons* in 1820 to warn the public of the many deceits practised upon them by food and drink fakers: alum in flour to whiten it, copperas in beer to give it 'a head', capsicum in mustard, dried leaves disguised as tea, spoiled cider rendered into 'wine' (wine faking was much more blatant then than now), and all the sins referred to in Chesterton's *Song against Grocers*, sand in sugar, dust in salt, tallow in butter, and so forth.

He was much hated by the bakers and brewers for his revelations and eventually supported in his fight by the *Lancet* and its 'scientific detective force',[1] as *Punch* called the contributors, who accused and named the manufacturers of chocolate enriched with brick-dust, the dairies who watered milk and then tinted it with chalk, the confectioners who used arsenical colorants. But it was forty years after Accum's book that the first Food and Drugs Act was passed.

Consumer protection is not new and by no means unnecessary (Accum gave examples of serious illnesses and deaths from adulterated food and drink). Those who assert that the modern citizen is well schooled enough to be able to make up his or her own mind are either being unbelievably naïve or taking up the position of Accum's opponents on *caveat emptor*, and it is of such thinking that the consumer knows he must beware. It is profoundly ironic that at a time when the United States, the free enterprise economy *par excellence*, is strengthening its government's hand against unfair manufacturing and trading practices, the British Government should decide to do exactly the opposite. But there has been no attempt as yet to repeal the Trade Descriptions Act, and the defunct Consumer Council will have its place taken by unsubsidized activity inspired by its past work, such as the *Sunday Times* consumer unit. Since this was written Sir Geoffrey Howe's consumer protection team at the Department

1. Nader's Raiders are not the first consumer vigilantes.

of Trade and Industry has come into being. This reversal of anti-consumer protection policy is very interesting in view of the arguments put forward here.

Those manufacturers and their managers who feel they should cheer at the demise of the Council should ask themselves why. No honest dealer, no sound products have ever been hurt by any of the consumer activity (if by sound we mean fit for purpose and of good quality). The Council of Industrial Design, which has sponsored some good-looking but unsound products, continues to receive Government money. A sensible move would have been to amalgamate the two and make the CoID more realistic.

All that may seem by the way, but it is not, for with or without Government support the individual consumer will continue to find ways and means of squaring up to the producer. Business itself has been known, albeit reluctantly sometimes, to discipline its own ranks. Price fixing is now illegal, here and elsewhere, for that came to be regarded as a form of business discipline that was not in the general interest. Economic history is rich in examples of non-competitive agreements (rings, combines, cartels, gentlemen's agreements) that eventually came to naught, but not until after the beneficiaries had added several noughts to their own net worth. The outstanding example that survives because it does not come under the law of any particular country is the International Air Transport Association, a conspiracy of airlines to fix routes, fares, and the quality of service, from the seat pitch (dimensions) to the number of vegetables served with a meal. The consumers of air travel and those of their suppliers who do not belong to IATA have found many ways round these restrictions, in spite of the support of governments (who own most of the member airlines) with restrictive legislation. The situation in airline operation has become very interesting for an outside observer. In spite of all these restrictions on consumer freedom of choice, few if any of them are making profits.

Lest it be felt that this is not a businesslike approach to product innovation let us say here and now that profit is the object of the exercise. But that profit will not accrue in the medium to long run if the paying customer is not taken care of. The sharp operator may seem to have the advantage in the short run, but it can only be short; perhaps three or four years at the most unless he is exceptionally lucky. In that time, of course, this sort of entrepreneur may have made enough money on which to retire. There are some examples to point to, but their exemplary nature suggests that they are exceptional rather than normal.

The business which is in business to stay needs to think further ahead and therefore needs to think in terms of cumulative customer reaction to its products or services. Your brand name does not become a household word any other way, unless it becomes the sort of word which households exchange as warnings. This still leaves a great many opportunities to take the public's money but, as we said at the beginning of this book, they are not worth discussing here. We are concerned with the failure rate of genuine product innovations and not with the compilation of a sucker's handbook. There is certainly room for one, but the modern law of libel leaves insufficient room for the kind of denunciation indulged in by Accum and the *Lancet.* It is possible to publish a *Good Food Guide* and to exclude restaurants of poor standard. Any attempt to publish a list of allegedly bad establishments would immediately lead to actions for libel, such as the one brought by a British restaurateur against the *Guide Julliard de Londres* after its 1965 edition had denounced his eating place for various reasons.

Paradoxically it is possible for critics to castigate plays, books, films, concerts, and other works of art without much fear of actions for libel (they have been known, for example the famous lawsuit against Mrs E. Arnot Robertson by MGM about thirty years ago). When *Which?* was launched with the avowed policy of criticizing products there were many who predicted that it would collapse under a shower of writs. A few threats have been made and one or two actions brought, but *Which?* has continued to represent the critical consumer, no doubt because, in spite of its vast circulation (over 600,000 in 1973) it is a membership publication and therefore 'private'.

Elsewhere, however, product criticism has to be guarded for fear of libel suits, although occasionally a Sunday newspaper has 'exposed' a small racketeer and put him out of business, knowing that he did not have the resources to counter-attack through the courts. Generally speaking the law of libel acts as a shield for business (it would have been regarded as unwise, for instance, to publish any suspicions that Vehicle and General, the motor insurance firm which went into liquidation in March 1971, was becoming insolvent, although many expert observers knew that it was). In addition most people believe, wrongly according to some legal opinion, that once a writ is issued the subject of a libel action becomes *sub judice* and therefore cannot be publicly discussed until the hearings are terminated. Thus have public discussions of dubious goods and services been silenced for years. In future this is much less likely to occur.

There are, then, two important marketing aspects of product innovation. With industrial goods there is the rather obvious necessity to involve potential users at as early a stage as possible, within the bounds of commercial discretion, of course. It is arguable, however, that commercial secrecy is overdone and can have more disadvantages than the simple one of letting the cat out of the bag. If a firm produces a new instrument or machine in absolute isolation it should not be surprised to find that its new product fails to make the right impact upon the market at which it has been aimed.

When Taylor, Taylor, and Hobson, the Leicester optical instrument manufacturers were working on the very successful Talyrond, an instrument for checking the precise roundness of machined parts and bearings, they showed R. E. Reason's working model to a group of potential users, including Rolls-Royce and Ransom & Marles. The instrument had been suggested by potential users in the first place, following the success of the Talysurf, an earlier device for measuring surface finish. 'Bill' Reason believes that keeping in close touch with users and with working conditions for such devices (some would term this 'close coupling' with the market) contributes greatly to the design of an acceptable product. It may seem obvious but how often is it done and done properly?

Burns and Stalker[1] found that too many years of working to the precise specifications of government departments deprived electronics firms of their 'feel' for the market. This is comparatively easy to put right in industrial innovation (provided that the defect is observed and admitted) by establishing close links with whatever markets seem to be appropriate to the innovation. The market itself will quickly indicate if it is interested or not.[2] The sad fact is that the absence of market knowledge, in the sense of fitting the product to the needs of the users (not adaptation but design), is so seldom fully realized. The author was shown an impressive analytical instrument

1. *The Management of Innovation* (Tavistock Publications, 1961).

2. An outline of industrial innovation management is sketched in Robertson, Andrew, *The Management of Industrial Innovation* (Industrial Educational and Research Foundation, 1969).

by its makers, who were proud of its advanced technology and convinced of its value to metallurgists and others. They had made a batch of twelve, but had not received a single order. Astonishingly they had neither demonstrated it at development or prototype stage, nor lent one to a potential user for evaluation under working conditions.

So, as we have noted, the discipline is severer in industrial innovation. With consumer products it is far less so, as we can observe from the extraordinarily large number of inappropriate products on sale. Yet the failure rate is higher in general than with industrial innovation. These associated phenomena can perhaps be explained by 'loose coupling' between makers and markets. On the one hand inappropriate products are launched, but find a market *faute de mieux* ('better than nothing'). On the other, still less acceptable products come on the market and either fail instantly or are withdrawn after a period of time during which the manufacturer has been urging his sales force on to 'move' them. The commonest explanation of new product failure in the past was 'poor salesmanship' and even the unfortunate salesmen believed it. Now, it is to be hoped, managers may find it possible to look at the total innovation sequence, not merely at the selling end.

As John Brooks pointed out in his essay on Xerox in *Adventures in Business*, it took users some time to realize that the copies of documents they were making with the 3M Thermofax copier were turning black and illegible in the files. While they were turning black more Thermofax copiers were being sold. Once the word got round that the copies did not last, the Thermofax was bound to fail, but many hundreds of thousands had been sold. If the production and design people are sometimes dazzled by apparent technological 'sweetness', the marketing people are also too easily convinced by sales figures (look back at the Vauxhall case, the Rolls washing machine case, and the Corfam case, for examples of this type of figuring), and consequently taken by surprise when a promising surge of sales peters out prematurely.

What the so-called 'consumer movement' does is to shorten the route and accelerate the feedback. It is to that extent a mixed blessing for the product innovator. If he is genuinely interested in innovating, and not merely pretending to innovate for the sake of short-term profit, he may find that this form of product testing is helpful in arriving at a worthwhile design and level of quality. Unfortunately, unless he has made almost identically rigorous tests himself at development stage, his product will already be in the factory and adaptation will be correspondingly costly (depending upon how extensive the modifications have to be to meet criticism). There have been numbers of occasions when *Which?* has reported that, for example, an electrical appliance has been rendered safe during the interval between submitting their report to its makers and publishing their findings in the magazine.

Incidentally, it is worth noting that the British Electrical Approvals Board came into being as a result of outside pressures on the industry to establish safety standards. It is one of several examples of self-discipline by an industry. Another is the Retail Trading-Standards Association which actually prosecutes companies (even its own members) in the textile trades who are found to have transgressed the law on descriptions and quality. Such organizations are not welcomed by the marginal firm, but are essential to the profitable conduct of firms which have an interest in quality and reliability as an element in ongoing corporate success and survival. It obviously costs more to make a product safe, reliable, and fit for purpose than to turn out a superficially attractive but inherently poor quality and possibly unsafe article; but if the price of the latter is significantly lower it will sell for just as long as the public takes to become aware of its deficiencies. Newspapers have a part to play in this, of course, but their crusading tends to be limited by their dependence on advertising revenue.

The 'media' have tended to bc vulnerable in this respect, but the papers which earn most of their income from sales have generally been bolder. The popular Sunday newspapers (notably the *People* and the *News of the World*) have campaigned on behalf of consumers, but not usually against the big firms who have for once indulged in some questionable activity, but rather against fly-by-night estate agents, dishonest doorstep or mail-order selling, and occasionally false or dangerous claims for such things as slimming pills or baldness cures. Nevertheless many papers which have carried consumer material (the late *Daily Sketch* was one such) have also published patent medicine advertisements, some of which could be regarded as, to put it nicely, optimistic.

The BBC tried 'consumerism' for a while with its television programme *Focus* and similar treatments of material from *Which?* on radio programmes like *Today*, but it was inclined to be presented in overwhelming detail to avoid charges of bias in favour of one brand name or another. Commercial television naturally takes the view that it cannot take sides against its advertisers, with the result that little or nothing that might be described as consumer advice has ever been attempted.

Nevertheless the media, usually under the guise of news, have provided short, fast feedback routes on occasions, and it is arguable that they could and should do more, and may yet, if encouraged in the right way. If they were to make the attempt again (and the new Insight consumer unit of the *Sunday Times* and the *Observer*'s plans to devote more space to consumer protection may be only the beginning) it could mean that a larger proportion of the buying public would be 'educated' in this way, and not just the ABs and part of the C1s as at present. However, most serious marketing people pay attention to the more affluent sections of the consuming public and, as we have noted earlier, they are being made more aware and more critical.

This summary of the critical aspects of the consumer products market provides minimal guidance to marketing people interested in the *strategy* of satisfaction, to cite the theme of this book. The word strategy is chosen for its long-term implications and because it figures in the title of Ernest Dichter's *Strategy of Desire*. We all know the feeling of desire, and we also know that not all desires once aroused are completely satisfied. The advertising industry, the light cavalry of the marketing army, concentrates on arousing desire: far too often by associating everything from pipe tobacco to steel with sex. There are no recorded cases of anyone obtaining sexual satisfaction from a tin of tobacco or a sheet of tinplate.

Cavalry is a tactical force, and may gain short-term positions for the marketing army. The consolidation of those positions is a matter of strategy involving every division from research and development to the front line of marketing. As other writers have remarked, there is an inherent danger in planning advertising to arouse desires that the actual product cannot begin to fulfil, and we are not necessarily harping on the ubiquitous sex theme: other motivating forces that advertisers have tried to employ include fear, particularly of social disapproval, snobbery, superficial social standing (identification of 'success' with possessions), family love, security in old age (or sickness, another facet of the fear motive), and in general to associate a product with happiness, contentment, and other comfortable mental states.

It follows that a sharp contrast between promise and product can only lead to a letdown for the consumer and that, strategically, is a mistake. At least we have some examples in this collection of cases of long-term disenchantment with the product leading to a downturn in sales (Cases 1 and 7 suggest this). Advertising protagonists will probably dispute the assertion that promise in the announcement has to be fulfilled in the product. After all, so many promises implicit in advertisements are incapable of fulfilment. (Will the girl who uses the toothpaste get the ski instructor? Will the young man with the executive suit get an executive job? Of course not, these are silly questions. But what about the statements?)

We all accept that these are unreal situations, that they are only ways of drawing attention to or keeping attention fixed on a product. There is, however, an inherent danger that the makers and vendors will pay more attention to the image of the product than to the product itself. All those images of virility associated with beer-drinking do not disguise the declining gravity strength of the various brews, which are coming to be more and more alike. There is every likelihood that the winner of future races for the greater share of a market will be the business which opts for a better product and honest advertising. At the worst it would be so different that it would be a publicity stunt in itself.

It is the author's fond hope that this collection of cases will be enlarged and extended as more material comes to light, but whether there will be any future editions at all will depend on the satisfaction generated by this product. However, if it only makes marketing people and others in business think twice it will have gone a long way.